Can Pop Culture and Shakespeare Exist in the Same Classroom?

Expecting students to jump right into a rigorous literature discussion is not always realistic. Students need scaffolding so that they will be more engaged and motivated to read the text and think about it on a deeper level. This book shows English language arts teachers a very effective way to scaffold—by tapping into students' interest in pop culture. You'll learn how to use your students' ability to analyze pop culture and transfer that into helping them analyze and connect to a text.

Special Features:

- Tools you can use immediately, such as discussion prompts, rubrics, and planning sheets
- Examples of real student literature discussions using pop culture
- Reflection questions to help you apply the book's ideas to your own classroom
- Connections to the Common Core State Standards for reading, speaking, and listening

Throughout the book, you'll discover practical ways that pop culture and classic texts can indeed coexist in your classroom. As your students bridge their academic and social lives, they'll become more insightful about great literature—and the world around them.

Kristine Gritter teaches pre-service and in-service teachers at Seattle Pacific University and is a former middle school language arts teacher.

Kathryn Schoon-Tanis is a professor of rhetoric and composition of popular culture at Hope College in Michigan. She was previously a high school English teacher.

Matthew Althoff is a principal at Seattle Christian Schools and a former middle school language arts teacher.

Other *Eye On Education* Books Available from Routledge
(www.routledge.com/eyeoneducation)

Writing Behind Every Door: Common Core Writing in the Content Areas
Heather Wolpert-Gawron

Rebuilding Research Writing: Strategies for Sparking Informational Inquiry
Nanci Werner-Burke, Karin Knaus, and Amy Helt DeCamp

Flipping Your English Class to Reach All Learners: Strategies and Lesson Plans
Troy Cockrum

Big Skills for the Common Core: Literacy Strategies for the 6–12 Classroom
Amy Benjamin and Michael Hugelmeyer

Teaching the Common Core Speaking and Listening Standards: Strategies and Digital Tools
Kristen Swanson

The Common Core Grammar Toolkit: Using Mentor Texts to Teach the Language Standards in Grades 3–5
Sean Ruday

The Common Core Grammar Toolkit: Using Mentor Texts to Teach the Language Standards in Grades 6–8
Sean Ruday

Authentic Learning Experiences: A Real-World Approach to Project-Based Learning
Dayna Laur

Nonfiction Strategies That Work: Do This—Not That!
Lori G. Wilfong

Vocabulary Strategies That Work: Do This—Not That!
Lori G. Wilfong

Common Core Literacy Lesson Plans: Ready-to-Use Resources, K–5
Common Core Literacy Lesson Plans: Ready-to-Use Resources, 6–8
Common Core Literacy Lesson Plans: Ready-to-Use Resources, 9–12
Edited by Lauren Davis

Teaching Students to Dig Deeper: The Common Core in Action
Ben Johnson

Can Pop Culture and Shakespeare Exist in the Same Classroom?

Using Student Interest to Bring Complex Texts to Life

Kristine Gritter,
Kathryn Schoon-Tanis,
and Matthew Althoff

Routledge
Taylor & Francis Group

NEW YORK AND LONDON

First published 2014
by Routledge
711 Third Avenue, New York, NY 10017

and by Routledge
2 Park Square, Milton Park, Abingdon, Oxon OX14 4RN

Routledge is an imprint of the Taylor & Francis Group, an informa business

Library of Congress Cataloging-in-Publication Data

Gritter, Kristine.
Can pop culture and Shakespeare exist in the same classroom? : using student interest to
  bring complex texts to life / by Kristine Gritter, Kathryn Schoon-Tanis, and Matthew Althoff.
     pages cm
  Includes bibliographical references.
  1. Language arts (Secondary)   2. Popular culture.   I. Schoon-Tanis, Kathryn.   II. Althoff,
Matthew.   III. Title.
  LB1631.G775   2014
  428.0071'2—dc23   2013043920

ISBN: 978-0-415-73469-1 (hbk)
ISBN: 978-0-415-73318-2 (pbk)
ISBN: 978-1-315-81981-5 (ebk)

Typeset in Optima
by Apex CoVantage, LLC

Contents

Acknowledgments ix

Meet the Authors xi

1 **A Different Way of Teaching Literature** 1

Developing Relational Stances With Texts Through Discussion 2

Reader Response Theory 6

Stages of Discussion 7

What the Research Says . . . and a Common Snafu 8

Dialogic Exchange 9

Permeable Textual Discussion 10

Opportunity for Reflection 14

2 **How to Improve Literature Discussions With Popular Culture** 15

Creating Rules for Discussion and Tracking Student Participation 16

Textual Discussion That Supports Balanced Literacy 17

Discussion Formats 19

Social Identities Matter! 22

What Is Popular Culture? And Why Does It Matter to ELA Teachers? 24

Popular Culture 27

Popular Culture in ELA 33

Opportunity for Reflection 34

3 **Literary Discussion and the Common Core State Standards** 35

The Point of Discussions 40

Introducing Matt: Middle School Language Arts Teacher 43

Opportunity for Reflection 46

4   Using Popular Culture as a Bridge to Complex Texts   47

Many Scholars Eschew Popular Culture in the Classroom   47
Teacher Views of Popular Culture Affect Teaching Practices   49
Alright, Enough Theory: How Do I Do This?   52
Thinking About Standards in a Broader Sense   57
Matt Uses Popular Texts as a Bridge to a Canonical Text   58
Opportunity for Reflection   65

5   What Rich Discussion Looks Like and How to Set It Up   67

A Bit More Background on Matt and a Situated Literature Unit   67
Girl Power Groups Demonstrate Rich Discussion   71
Did the Girl Power Group Meet Matt's Learning Targets?   79
Assessing Discussion   80
Opportunity for Reflection   88

6   Successful Discussions and Classroom Democracy in Action   91

Vignettes of Class Discussions   91
Opportunity for Reflection   107

7   Pop Culture and Media Literacy   109

Defining Media Literacy   110
How Media Literacy Occurs Through Discussions   111
Ways to Help Students Understand How Mass Media Work   113
Putting It All Together   115
Opportunity for Reflection   116

References   117

Acknowledgments

From Kathryn Schoon-Tanis:

This book would not have come to fruition without the dedication and commitment of Dr. Kristine Gritter. Throughout the process, she kept us all on task. I have never been so thankful for hearing, "Hey! You're a pop culture person!" Thank you.

I am also grateful for the ELA teachers who have, and who continue to, inspire my teaching and my work. For Amy, Meg, Sara, Stephanie, and Matt I am forever thankful. You all keep me going. Thank you.

Finally, to Lauren Davis, editor extraordinaire: Thank you!

Meet the Authors

Kristine Gritter was a middle school language arts teacher for several years before she decided she had so many questions about literacy teaching that she decided to go back to school to learn more about teaching and learning. She attended Michigan State University and graduated in 2007 with a Ph.D. with an emphasis in adolescent literacy. She now teaches pre-service and in-service teachers at Seattle Pacific University. She is thankful to have a career working with some of the best human beings in the universe: secondary teachers.

Kathryn Schoon-Tanis was a high school English teacher (and track and field coach) before she decided to pursue her questions about the relationship between popular culture and elite/high culture. She graduated with a Ph.D. in Curriculum, Instruction, and Teacher Education from Michigan State University in 2010. Since then, she has been teaching college courses examining the rhetoric and composition of popular culture for the English Department at Hope College in Holland, Michigan. When she is not teaching, she is trying to figure out a good rationale for her love of detective fiction, police procedurals, and the television show *New Girl*.

Matt Althoff was a middle school language arts teacher for 11 years before moving into administration. He is currently serving in his first year as principal at Seattle Christian Schools, placing a priority on teacher collaboration and professional development. He is grateful for his amazing wife and kids, and for all of the inspiring teachers and students with whom he has had the pleasure to work.

1 A Different Way of Teaching Literature

When we were training to be English language arts (ELA) teachers, little emphasis was placed on how to facilitate rich and lively literature discussions. Much more emphasis was placed on *the* meaning of literature, the authors of great literature, our professors' great insights, and even on our own understandings of literature. Our knowledgeable (often white, grizzled, male, pipe-smoking, tweed jacketed) English professors had privileged points of view. If they had an opinion or interpretation about a literary text, we wrote it down. It might be on the test. Or their interpretation might be useful if we ever taught the book to students. Our understanding of literature was filtered through the insights of experts.

This way of reading, talking about, and understanding literature worked for us as teachers if we taught the same texts we had studied in college and if we had intrinsically motivated students. In our early years of teaching, it was comfortable to direct students to the same literary insights and conclusions we learned from our professors. It made us feel educated and safe. We could unlock the secrets of great literature because we had studied at the feet of literary masters. Although we did not know it, we were practicing pedagogies of a literary school of thought called New Criticism, a philosophy that advocates close, detached readings of literature and rejects personal interpretation on the part of the reader.

But this approach did not always work for our secondary students. We were middle class, white, intrinsically motivated pre-service teachers careful to maintain our grade point averages. But some of our students did not care about grades and many did not care about the literature we assigned. They could make this painfully obvious on doodled reading quizzes and classroom behaviors (Kristine remembers a seventh grader sticking carrots up his nose as his class studied John Steinbeck's *The Red Pony*). New Criticism teaching practices did not reach many of our students. What worked for us as English majors training to be teachers was not working for all of our students. We learned—sometimes in difficult ways—that what students may need to do for literature to come alive is to develop relationships with text as they develop relationships with their peers.

Developing Relational Stances With Texts Through Discussion

The following student discussion characterizes students who are starting to develop relationships with a particular text, *A Wrinkle in Time*. Roxy, Caroline, Dana, and Tiana are discussing how they can relate to, or visualize, various characters. Note how they use popular culture as a gateway to understanding.

Roxy: I'm like Meg, Charles Wallace, and Mrs. Whatsit. I'm kind of like Charles because I like to know words that people don't. I'm like Meg because I'm a little clumsy. I'm like Mrs. Whatsit because sometimes people think I'm a little crazy.

Caroline: So I thought Meg was kind of like Frodo Baggins from *Lord of the Rings* because Bilbo's parental figure goes away mysteriously, and Meg's father goes away mysteriously. And Frodo tries to figure out how he goes away in a different manner than Meg.

Dana: She kind of related to me like Charlie Brown because Charlie Brown is kind of like Meg because he's quiet and shy and . . . but . . . Meg's not as shy. He's kind of like Charles Wallace instead. And Meg's kind of like Lucy where she's not afraid to say something and she wants to say it.

Tiana: I kind of think Charles Wallace is like one of those scary movies when there's a kid in this haunted house and everything about them, you don't even know them.

To want to read, one must have positive relationships with books. Judith Langer (1990) calls relationships with texts "stances" with reading. They deepen over time *if* readers invest their time and self in what they are reading. Langer believes that stances are developed as readers "move" through a text, although movement can retrace previous stances or move into new stances.

Langer describes an initial stance toward reading as "Being Out and Stepping Into an Envisionment." Readers in this stance use their prior knowledge and experiences to "walk" into a text as they initially try to make sense of it. (And, by the way, a text need not be a literary text; it might refer to a visual or auditory work of art like a movie or painting or song that can be analyzed and interpreted for deeper meaning.) Readers who step into an envisionment ask questions about what they are reading and come to a basic understanding of what the author is trying to say. In the above transcript, Roxy, Caroline, Dana, and Tiana have been cued by their teacher to step into an envisionment when he has asked them two open-ended questions: (1) How are you like characters you have encountered in the first few chapters of A Wrinkle in Time? (2) What connections can you make between the characters you encountered in this text and characters you encountered in other books or movies?

In a second stance, in which Langer describes as "Being In and Moving Through an Envisionment," readers move deeper into the text by making text-to-world, text-to-text, and text-to-self connections and seeing themselves in the text. If you have observed readers in public places cry or laugh because they are metaphorically "in" the book they are reading, you have seen this stance in action. The connections Roxy and friends make about A Wrinkle in Time show that they are moving through the first few chapters of the book. They are playing their own screenplay in their mind about the characters they have encountered (notice how the genres of their movies or television shows vary widely from fantasy to science fiction to cartoons).

Langer describes a third stance as "Stepping Back and Rethinking What One Knows." This occurs when readers have walked through a text and think about what it means. The readers then allow their interpretations of text to further shape their knowledge of self or the world. In the following discussion, students explore the themes of A Wrinkle in Time and themes in superhero movies and collectively reach conclusions about essential differences between superheroes and villains. Nolan, a seventh-grade student, is in the front of the class leading a whole-class discussion.

Nolan: Just like Superman had his Kryptonite, do you think, like, in the story, like, Meg and Charles have some weakness? Neo?

Neo: I think their weakness is fear of what could happen to their father.

Nolan: James?

James: I think Meg's weakness is Charles because she likes him so much and she would do anything for him.

As James notes, sometimes love might not be construed as a character's strength; this out-of-the-box thinking is considered sophisticated in adults, let alone in seventh graders. Loving too much might interfere with one's own rights or the rights of a collective group— an environment where novel thinking tends to lead to more of the same. Chelle, a classmate of Nolan, Neo, and James, has a related point to make about the book and superhero movies: Sometimes a character's physical weakness is the flaw that allows the plot to unfold. Neo observes that willpower could be construed by ordinary mortals as a weakness.

Chelle: Charles's weakness is probably physical strength. Like, he doesn't seem very physically strong as opposed to Meg, who's constantly getting in

> fights. . . . So Charles's [weakness] would be, like, if someone were to beat
> him up.

Neo, too, has an original point to make that doesn't make sense for his classmates at
first. Nonetheless, his teacher gives him the time and space to explain.

Neo: I think another weakness for the people is their willpower.
Students: What?

When Neo defends the point he is attempting to make with textual evidence from
A Wrinkle in Time, he shows he has rethought what everyone thought was true: that
willpower is always a virtue.

Neo: Because the superheroes we were mentioning, their strength is their will to
           fight. And Meg and Charles Wallace's will doesn't seem as strong. Because
           that's why Charles got hypnotized.
Nolan: Do you think the other side, the bad side, has weaknesses?
Harry: Well, like, IT [a character] has the weakness from love.
Neo: I just have to say that every villain has a weakness because villains do
           things because of the things that have happened to them and they feel like
           they need to take revenge on the things that have happened to them and
           that they're scared and frightened. And they want revenge to make every-
           body else feel like that. That's why they become villains.
Chelle: IT must have a weakness because he was beat by Meg. So if he were, like,
           immortal and didn't have a weakness, then obviously she would not have
           been able to beat him.
Neo: Oh, and another thing. Just to add to my point that villains do things
           because, like, someone makes fun of them, that's why they become a
           villain. For Batman . . . I mean the Riddler. He became the Riddler because
           of people making fun of his ideas. And that's why he became evil and stuff.

These students are engaged in rethinking what they know. Love, creativity, and
light are the essence of superheroes, the group decides. Hate, conformity, and darkness are the essence of villains. The setting of Camazotz, where all characters must
behave the same, allows evil and a villain to flourish. The cross-talk of students comparing characters in their literature with superheroes and villains in comic books and
movies allows them to think new thoughts about character flaws. These students discover that flaws can be more complicated than they appear at first glance. Thus they
are using discussion as a tool for rethinking.

New learning reshapes prior knowledge until knowledge is restructured. Langer
calls a fourth stance "Stepping Out and Objectifying the Experience." In this stance,

readers become critical and evaluative and can assess the worth of a text. In the following discussion, students critique the literary worth of *A Wrinkle in Time*:

Chase: It's kind of funny how they [the children in the novel] can go throughout their day and just be happy in their rickety, literally two-hundred-year-old house. It's kind of cool how they can just take what they have and put it into something good. That's a huge inspiration.

Caroline: I think that adds to the timeless quality of the book. [Looking at the front of the book for the copyright date]. They say it was written in 1962.

Chase: If you take this book and compare it to other books written back then, it's still in the top 50 books most purchased.

Caroline: Because the characters are easy to identify with . . . Meg.

Louis: And like the twins, they seem like lots of sports players that stick up for their family.

Caroline: You can tell this author had a childhood. Some of these authors write really static characters.

Louis, Caroline, and Chase feel *A Wrinkle in Time*, though written in 1962, is still talkworthy. Social-reject characters can still be related to 50 years later even if they live in rickety houses and do not have access to technology. In fact, Meg's creativity in "making do" without a cell phone or the Internet inspires Chase. After reading the book, these readers have moved through envisionment so they can categorize a book they have read as a quality text.

Unfortunately, struggling adolescent readers may not gain entrance into text and may not gain envisionment of text. Purcell-Gates (1991) observes that remedial readers are often in a fifth stance, "On the Outside Looking In," unable to make meaning of a text, reading but not understanding.

Literature discussions are one of the best mediating activities for teachers to prevent students from taking on this fifth stance, but New Criticism is no way for struggling readers to move through text. They must find entrance into text by making personal connections to literature. This means that instructional time must be designated for literature discussion, no small feat when teachers never seem to have enough time in the day. In addition, a rich discussion is characterized by text-to-self, text-to-world, text-to-other, and text-to-text connections uttered by students. Such a classroom environment means that teachers must have a sense of what students know in their home and school literary lives or want to know about the prior knowledge students bring to their school reading. It also means that teachers become facilitators for discussion—not dictators of discussion—knowing when to shape discussion through well-timed questions and clarifications and knowing when to move out of discourse space to let students shape discussion. Knowledge of a new theory for literary learning is necessary to create such an environment. Enter Reader Response Theory.

Reader Response Theory

Several decades ago, the grande dame of reading research, Louise Rosenblatt, articulated a rival concept to New Criticism that is our theoretical underpinning for advocating literature discussions that reference popular culture. Rosenblatt called her construct Reader Response Theory—a literary theory with rich pedagogical implications that can be seen in some English language arts classrooms today (in our opinions, some of the most dynamic English language arts classrooms). Back in 1938, Rosenblatt, a Reformed Jew whose religious tradition allowed her to interpret her religion through modern lenses, wrote a book she entitled *Literature as Exploration*. Rosenblatt believed that reading literature should be an active process where authentic thinking is encouraged and valued. Good reading entails self-knowledge and meta-cognition of personal interpretation while reading.

Louise Rosenblatt, who was still attending National Conference of Teachers of English conferences in 2004 when she was 101, observed that readers are active agents in the process of literary reading. They are as vital in the act of reading as authors and the words on the page. She asserted that books do not become powerful until readers make them powerful. Rosenblatt observed that powerful readers make sense of texts in terms they already know. Rather than relying on a teacher or critic to "spoonfeed" a single, standard interpretation of a text, students using Reader Response lenses construct their own meaning by connecting texts to issues in their lives. There is no one "right" answer or "correct" interpretation of a text according to this theory (although the notion of supplying textual evidence to defend your claim is part of active reading). The diverse responses of individual readers are key to discovering the variety of possible meanings a poem, story, essay, or other text can evoke. The Reader Response classroom celebrates multiple interpretations and gives voice to them during class time through textual discussions.

Louise Rosenblatt (1968) described a "transaction" of reading as "the synthesis of what the reader already knows and feels and desires and what the literary text offers—the patterned sensations, emotions, and ideas through which the author has sought to communicate his sense of life" (pp. 272–73). As we read, we are shaped by our culture. Powerful readers know this; but they are also interested in the culture from which texts emerge. Louis, Caroline, and Chase can "walk through" *A Wrinkle in Time* because their teacher has made sure that the cultural differences between their lives and Meg's life are not insurmountable. The cultural scaffolding we will demonstrate in future chapters allows the words on the page to take on meaning for the adolescent readers.

Rosenblatt describes a choice of two stances as students read: an "aesthetic stance," which is a very personal, open-ended response to literature, and an "efferent stance," involving a search for the right answer or a closed response. We were generally taught to read literature using an efferent response (our closed responses being correlated with what we thought our professors wanted us to know). But for literature to come alive for many of our students, we needed to help them develop aesthetic stances to literature. We have seen students develop aesthetic stances in the vignettes so far because of the cues they received from their teacher, Matthew.

Discussions are tools to facilitate aesthetic reading of text. During rich discussion, students use "exploratory talk" (Wilson & Laman, 2007) to work through their interpretations of text. There can be a social justice dimension to such exploratory talk if a teacher cues discussion in that direction: Students can ultimately come to personal and relevant conclusions about issues of social justice in the worlds of text and the world they live in. But they need freedom of interpretation to do so. Worksheets asking students to retell what has been stated in the text is not a conduit for exploratory talk. Open-ended questions such as, "What is happening here?" "Why is it happening here?" and "How do you personally relate to this event?" scaffold exploratory talk. Questions defending right or wrong in characters' actions promote the talk of social justice.

Stages of Discussion

Golden (2001) observes, "A text has different phases in its life. Individual reading presents one phase and group discussion of the text a second phase. The group text incorporates several individual texts. Talk among participants helps individuals confirm, extend, or modify their individual interpretations and create a better understanding of text" (p. 95). Great discussion doesn't just happen; it is a layered process. First, as Golden observes, a reader must comprehend the text. The outer layer of discussion works first at understanding the literal content of text. In a truly democratic textual discussion, students are given permission to identify textual information themselves that aids in literal comprehension. Before the discussion, they prepare questions they have about passages or select talkworthy or unclear passages to navigate with a small group. The following prompts allow for establishing literal comprehension of a text in a small group:

(1) I'm not sure what this word/passage on p. _____ means, but I think it might be important.

(2) I think this word/passage on p. _____ means _____ because of these clues:

(3) I think this word/passage on p. _____ may be important because of these clues:

(4) My one-sentence summary of this passage would be:

(5) After hearing the summaries of group members, my restated summary of this passage is:

A second stage of discussion involves textual interpretation. Some deeper Reader Response questions that trigger deeper thought might include the following:

(1) I think the paragraph on p. _____ is the most important paragraph in this chapter because it means _____.

(2) I really relate to this passage on p. _____ because _____.

(3) When I read the passage on p. _____, I felt _____.

(4) I agree/disagree with _____, because I believe _____.

(5) I can make a prediction that _____ will happen in this text because of the following evidence:

What the Research Says . . . and a Common Snafu

Language arts teachers enacting Reader Response instructional practices in their classrooms look for ways students can actively interpret texts in ways other than discussion. Teaching practices might include student journaling while reading and peer editing groups in which student authors explain their writing choices. Research has shown that students in Reader Response–based classrooms read more and make richer personal connections with texts than students using more traditional methods (Langer, 2001). Students in Reader Response classrooms tend to be more tolerant of multiple interpretations of texts, a necessary skill in the pluralistic society in which we live. Students can learn techniques that help them recognize the ways in which their own arguments are formed because Reader Response techniques analyze culture and rhetorical choices authors make when constructing texts. Students become better equipped to examine the arguments of others. In short, Reader Response helps students to become better critical readers and become a community of readers.

The problem with Reader Response Theory is that students may not always have equally valid or appropriate responses to text during discussion. Some students may have comprehension issues with a text, so they cannot interpret the text well. Some students enjoy the sound of their own voice and speak without thinking. Some students can veer off the text onto unrelated tangents, commandeering discussion in ways that a teacher cannot anticipate or does not map onto learning targets.

The meaning of a text is not an entirely subjective matter. Good readers of diverse cultural backgrounds often uniformly decide on themes of a text because of commonalities of the human experience. It is crucial that responses to a text be buttressed by evidence from the text itself and from the context in which the text is read.

Ultimately, however, the most important aspect of a Reader Response classroom is that each member—gifted reader, struggling reader, or classroom teacher—goes beyond his or her first response to assimilate the points of view of others in the class if others make valid arguments. Even though an individual reader's reactions are based on his or her own "schema" (the expectations that arise from personal experiences or existing knowledge), he or she should realize in class discussion that not everyone shares that same perspective. This knowledge is an important construct in democracy and scaffolds students to live in a pluralistic society where multiple points of view on complicated topics are expected and liberal discourse prevails even when conversationalists do not share the same opinions.

Two constructs are important when describing excellent literature discussion: dialogic exchange and permeable textual discussion. Before we continue, we would like to define these two constructs.

Dialogic Exchange

Dialogic exchange (Nystrand, 1997) is literature classroom talk that is conversational and explorative. Teachers and students, especially students, are in dialogue around a text. In dialogic exchange, students ask deep questions of a text, build on each other's responses, and become co-teachers to each other. In dialogic discussion, a teacher facilitates classroom talk to maintain an order and structure but does not dominate textual talk. In fact, in dialogic exchange, students often self-select to speak or ask questions of other students rather than fielding questions asked by the teacher. Although the teacher, as perhaps a more expert reader, has some goal of the direction of shared knowledge, teachers and students can negotiate subtopics of discussion. So teachers facilitating dialogic exchange tend to ask open ended questions with no one specific right answer. Eventually students involved in dialogic exchange should learn to ask open-ended questions of each other as well.

In a dialogic classroom, important questions are documented and turned into organizing frameworks for ongoing lessons or discussions. Dialogic exchange looks more like a book club of social equals than typical recitation in an English language arts classroom. As Nystrand (1997) concludes, "Successful teachers follow their students' voices . . . listening carefully and opening dialogue. Phrasing instruction according to students' abilities, interests, and experiences, they take their students seriously, finding—sometimes creating—ways to let their students know that what they think counts" (p. 108). Dialogic exchange invites student questions and ideas into discussion. It is truly *student centered*, an attribute of pedagogy many teachers endorse but may not practice as much as they might.

A dialogic classroom looks and feels a certain way. Student questions and responses to literature line the wall and are the heart of the literary curriculum. Instead of completing worksheets supplied by textbook companies, students record their own questions encountered while reading. They also record their findings—and those of their peers. Students decide if they can reach consensus on big social justice issues that are provoked by a text. If they cannot, they document why they cannot agree using culturally sensitive language.

Permeable Textual Discussion

During permeable textual discussions, students make connections to texts based on their prior knowledge of themselves, the world, and previous literature (Gritter, 2012). This concept comes from the work of Anne Haas Dyson, who realized that primary grade students wrote layered, interesting stories when they brought their prior knowledge of superheroes, sports, television shows, and their social worlds into their writing. She called this a *permeable curriculum*. In her research, a permeable curriculum results in better writers and comprehenders of text because teachers, students, and parents come to understand that children already know a great deal of how the world works (Dyson, 1997, 2003). Tapping into this knowledge creates verisimilitude (Barnes, 1993), considering the characters, places, and events of literature as real.

In her beautifully descriptive book, *The Girl With the Brown Crayon*, Vivian Paley (1997) allows a gifted African American kindergarten student to help craft a yearlong literature exploration of Leo Leonni's picture books based on her understandings of race, community, and the personal motivation and gifts of classmates. Although Paley does not reveal her pedagogy much in this book, it does provide weighty examples of rich literature discussion with a focus student. The literary and social insights of Paley's kindergarten class are sophisticated and far above the level of most adult expectations of young students. Paley's students, especially her focal student Reeny, does the work of critical literacy, examining justice and injustice as she reads deeply and interprets Leo Leonni's books. Teachers can work toward creating permeable textual discussions that address critical literacy by collecting, and having students collect, classroom data informing the following questions:

- What personal connections are students making to the text?
- What questions are they asking of each other and the text?
- In what ways are they identifying or empathizing with the characters' plights?
- In what ways are they critiquing the text and the world? Who gets to tell "the story"? Who does not get to tell the story?
- What are the exchanges (who gets to speak and what is their position on matters of social justice)? (Wilson & Laman, 2007, p. 45)

Existing literacy theory and research advocate permeable textual talk in English language arts classrooms for adolescents (Keene & Zimmerman, 1997). Langer's (2001) research indicates that secondary classrooms that demonstrate high-level literacy ability are led by teachers who offer adolescents opportunities for multiple texts to be deconstructed and discussed. In these "beating the odds" classrooms—classrooms of economically disadvantaged students who nonetheless demonstrate sophisticated literacy skill as measured on assessment data—adolescents relate personally to print and connect it to their own lives. Morgan (1998) describes the personal and intertextual connections that discerning language teachers scaffold in order to bring the identities of adolescents into reading tasks: creating room for dialogue concerning the cultural and ideological power relations that shape literary characters; giving adolescents the freedom to read against text if it contradicts the reader's worldview; and addressing gaps and silences in texts. This book will offer multiple methods and resources for leading students to richer literary examination through discussion referencing popular culture.

Why Use Popular Culture to Create a Permeable Curriculum?

Similar to the way English language arts teachers wonder how best to incorporate rich textual discussions, they also often wonder how to create or enhance positive relationships with the classic, canonical texts of the ELA classroom to create a permeable curriculum. As English majors—people naturally interested in reading and discussing literature—ELA teachers often have a kind of innate love of literature; for many teachers, reading (and discussing) comes naturally and easily, which is not the case for many of the students who come into our classrooms. Wanting students to develop a positive relationship with texts from the literary canon and knowing that rich discussion is a tool to promote such a positive relationship are not easy stances to establish as ELA teachers.

The question remains: How do we, as ELA teachers, effectively incorporate rich literature discussions? Throughout this book, we argue that one of the best ways to promote discussion—to activate prior knowledge, to ask questions, to make connections, to think about meaning, to become critical and evaluative—is by using texts (characters, stories, settings, themes, and so on) from popular culture to discuss texts from the literary canon. However, like a lack of preparation in leading discussion, there has been seemingly little in teacher education to prepare teachers for using texts from popular culture in the ELA classroom, including methods of adopting strategies for responding to students when they naturally incorporate popular texts into classroom discussion or writing. ELA teachers often hesitate incorporating popular texts into class discussions because of the assumption that English education needs to be about upholding the transmission of culture through restricting reading and discussion to the canonical texts (Shakespeare, Steinbeck, Miller, Hawthorne, Hemingway, Frost, Fitzgerald—"the dead white guys"). There seems to be the notion that if a teacher includes a text from popular culture, then that teacher is both *replacing* a canonical text with a popular text as well as *demeaning* the superior nature of the canon with the lesser nature of popular culture. As one teacher commented:

> I think I'm conflicted about [popular culture], especially when I think about using it in my classroom. . . . I love the idea of having something to bring into my classroom that my students can relate to and make connections across modern, and, you know, more canonical texts, depending on what I'm teaching. . . . Basically, and when I say that I'm conflicted about pop culture, again, it's like how much *value* does it really have? And that's a question I have. I have doubts about it. But yet I feel like I'm in a position where I often have to defend my use of it even though I too stand on the other side of the argument sometimes. (Schoon-Tanis, 2010, p. 81, emphasis added)

The tension of simultaneously wanting to include texts with which students are familiar and wondering about the academic value of such texts pervades the literature written about using popular culture texts in secondary ELA (Allender, 2004; Cawelti, 2004; Morrell, 2002). Including popular texts is a potentially frightening move given the emphasis and value we place on canonical texts. But we also can't ignore what students already know and what students already can do. In fact, knowing what students already know is the biggest teaching asset available for teachers.

But can we consider the possibility that a teacher can use a text from popular culture *with* a text from the literary canon? If popular texts can work with canonical texts to enhance and offer insights, suggest connections, and evoke critical thinking, then, we argue, teachers should use them! This way of incorporating popular texts (texts that students naturally refer to in the classroom) can be a way of honoring the classic literary canon by using the popular text to draw attention to the canonical text by presenting a deeper understanding and a richer appreciation.

Incorporating popular texts in literary discussions is not easy. We acknowledge that trying to incorporate the constant changes that occur in popular culture and the changes that occur in the technology that drives popular culture into a curriculum is fraught with difficulty. Teachers generally are not of the same generation as their students and may pay attention to different facets of popular culture. It is nearly impossible, especially for nondigital natives, to keep up-to-date and current with technological trends, especially in cash-strapped schools. Additionally, it is difficult to find an "expert" from whom to find guidance and insight when seeking appropriate popular texts to incorporate. When teaching canonical texts, ELA teachers have decades of scholarship (scholarly writing, lesson and unit plans, lecture notes from university classes, and so on) from which to draw. This isn't always the case with popular texts. The popularity—and accessibility—of texts is constantly changing. Just look at the phenomenon of popular music where one song/artist is rarely popular from one year to the next. ("Rolling in the Deep" by Adele was the most popular song in 2011; "Call Me Maybe" by Carly Rae Jepsen was the most popular song in 2012. And while both songs were the "most popular" of their year, many people, in eliciting a kind of cultural hierarchy, would argue that the two artists couldn't be more different in that Adele has more "staying power" and talent than Carly Rae Jepsen, thus adding another complicating layer to the constant shifts in popular culture.) As Hagood, Alvermann, and Heron-Hruby (2010) write:

> [It] can be hard to 'wrap your mind around' a text that may have been banned in schools (like a graphic novel) or that wasn't defined as text (like a film) only a few years ago and is now promoted as central to the curriculum! Yet most educators can agree that the texts of our day-to-day lives have rapidly changed in the past 10 years, and technology has forever altered how we interact with one another and learn about ourselves and the world. (p. 3)

The constant shifting and changing nature of technology and of popular culture makes it nearly impossible to keep up-to-date on what students find interesting and makes it difficult to find current examples of popular texts that work well with canonical texts. Incorporating popular texts into the ELA classroom seems a daunting task.

Finally, there are many who say that popular culture should be restricted to what students do outside of the classroom—the classroom should be a place where students are exposed to "the best that has been thought and said" (Arnold, 1869, qtd. in Guins & Cruz, 2005, p. 4). Hagood and colleagues (2010) challenge this notion by suggesting that teachers need to

> reflect on long-held beliefs . . . that informal learning is separated, often by school walls from formal learning; that print is the mode of choice for communicating in the classroom; and that only people with low-brow tastes engage with pop culture, while the rest of us 'educated' folks distance ourselves from television, comic books, and the like. (p. 2)

It is no longer possible to ignore the fact that what students *know* is popular culture. It is no longer possible to disregard the fact that students *connect* the characters and stories they know from popular texts to the literary canon that they experience in the classroom. (As an aside, it is also no longer possible for us "educated" ELA teachers to hide the fact that we, too, engage popular culture. It may look like a different engagement than our students' engagement, but it is still an active engagement.)

We want students to become critical consumers of texts as well as a part of a community of readers (and writers, discussers, and listeners) working together to expand perspectives. If teachers create, and maintain, a strong division between what happens outside of the classroom and what happens inside of the classroom, then they restrict the potential connections students can make. They limit and constrain the potential for critical thinking, insightful reasoning, and effective collaboration—all traits that students in the 21st century must have.

Opportunity for Reflection

Consider how you might apply the ideas from this chapter to your own classroom.

1. How do you develop a relationship with a text as you read?

2. How do you encourage your students to develop a relationship with texts?

3. Describe permeable text discussions in your own words. Are they happening in your class? How might you encourage them?

4. How can pop culture help?

5. What are your concerns about using pop culture in the classroom?

How to Improve Literature Discussions With Popular Culture

2

In Chapter 1, we included a few brief vignettes featuring students discussing *A Wrinkle in Time* in their language arts class. Their words illustrate that discussions allow students to develop deeper envisionment with literature. In future chapters we will describe how allowing students to demonstrate connections with literature based on their prior knowledge of popular culture leads to unexpected discoveries in literature. This is a nuts-and-bolts chapter. That is, in this chapter we would like to summarize research that indicates that literature discussions are a best practice in English language arts (ELA) classrooms. We would also like to describe how teachers could organize discussions. Finally, we would like to be explicit in our understanding of popular culture. It is a highly contested term, so definitions matter and have consequences for teaching.

Literature discussions, sadly, are not a common practice in secondary schools. In one two-year study of hundreds of eighth- and ninth-grade English classrooms in a variety of settings (urban, suburban, rural, public, parochial), discussion lasted 50 seconds in eighth grade and less than 15 seconds in ninth grade (Nystrand, 1997, p. 33). The lower the track and the poorer the students, the less likely students discussed the texts that they were reading. Nystrand's study concluded that 20 percent of student responses during textual talk involved students answering a teacher question with a one-word yes or no response. If a major goal for the teaching of learning of ELA is for students to develop a democratic voice that they will use in democracy, this is a disturbing find.

There is a difference between recitation and discussion. Recitation involves what is called an Initiation-Response-Evaluation (I-R-E) pattern, in which a teacher selects a student speaker and asks him or her a recall-type question, the student responds (usually briefly), providing an answer to the question, and the teacher evaluates the correctness of the student response (Cazden, 2001). These conversational volleys tend to be brief, to focus on literal comprehension of text, and to reinforce teaching to test questions where there is one right response to be regurgitated later on a summative assessment. This kind of practice hardly values—or validates—the students' prior knowledge or incorporates peers into digging deeper into text.

Creating Rules for Discussion and Tracking Student Participation

Almasi (1995) and Eeds and Wells (1989) conclude that discussion is best when a teacher facilitates textual talk. Discussion can be best characterized as student-dominated textual talk that encourages students to solve textual problems and leads to greater small-group or class comprehension of that literature. Facilitators of discussion must be savvy, however, in leading students to problem solving and deeper comprehension. Maloch (2002) describes how one teacher adroitly scaffolded student talk in literature discussions over time. The classroom teacher, Ms. P, had to explicitly tell students they had to connect wholes from each other's conversational turns and not just share personal insights. She instituted rules and strategies for discussion that are worth sharing for optimal discussion (Maloch, p. 103). Here are Ms. P's rules for discussion:

- All members must be involved and included, even shy students.
- Group members should share their response to text.
- Group members should invite others to share, value, and acknowledge other student turns by asking follow-up questions, restating what group members had said, and thanking group members for sharing something particularly interesting. Active listening is a valuable part of participating in democracy and should not be undervalued by the group.
- Students should talk to each other and not to the teacher when she is present. That means students should maintain eye contact with other group members and show through body language that they are engaged in active listening.
- Discussion turns need to be connected across turns as group members ask follow-up questions or expand on others' turns.
- Students must generate topics for discussion that are important. They should argue why their topic is important.
- Students should refer to literature, especially page numbers and particular passages, for deeper understanding of text.
- Students should build on previous discussions across time.
- Discussions should work with a book's main themes.

- Personal connections should be considered the most important kinds of sharing.

- Students might need to retell a story or anecdote in text so that everyone can reference the same background knowledge. That might entail turning to the actual passage.

- Students should alert group members when they are getting off track.

- Students should not just give a literal restatement of what they read; they should extend their talk to discuss what a passage actually means.

- Over time, the teacher should talk less and observe students engage in the rules and strategies.

We would like to add that showing students how to document discussions (i.e., recording memorable student discussion turns from members in the group and documenting topics for discussion and eventual conclusions to discussion) allows teachers (and students) to assess what is happening in discussions and how thinking has changed as the result of group interpreting and sharing literature. Teachers can create discussion charts with a coding system to track a classroom discussion: O (original question or comment), F (follow-up question or comment), P (personal story or connection), R (retelling or restating a textual passage), # (page numbers of passage referenced), and open-ended summaries responding to a teacher- or student-generated prompt before and after the discussion.

We have found that these rules are helpful in creating dialogic and permeable textual discussion and should be explicitly explained to students a few at a time, published for students so they can be referenced over time, and added to throughout the school year.

Textual Discussion That Supports Balanced Literacy

As we observed earlier, we think that discussion can teach students to be better comprehenders of text, so we support textual discussion that supports balanced literacy. That is to say, there are different methods of textual discussion that serve different purposes. Balanced literacy instruction integrates pleasurable language instruction with the use of quality and culturally and developmentally relevant texts and explicit instruction in the teaching of the skills of good readers (Pressley, Roehrig, Bogner, Raphael, & Dolezal, 2002). Struggling readers who are on "the outside looking in" on textual discussion need to learn how to read even as they discuss literature. They can learn the strategies of good reading during textual discussion.

Good readers are different than struggling readers. They have a plan as they read: They have a purpose for reading, they know when they are comprehending and when they are not, and they have an arsenal of strategies to fix their confusion. Reading strategies that aid comprehension include the following:

- activating prior knowledge
- identifying succinctly what is most important in a passage
- excluding less important information that may be confusing
- asking clarifying questions of self and author
- making text-to-text connections of other texts of the same author, genre, or historical period
- creating a mental movie of what is happening in the text and describing that movie in terms of sensory details described in the text, including sights, tastes, smells, sounds, and sensations of touch
- reading in-between the lines to make inferences about the text using prior knowledge
- often synthesizing what is read by adding important new information to summaries as more is read and new information is revealed by the author
- using a variety of fix-it strategies to repair comprehension: skipping ahead of a confusing passage, rereading, using the context to figure out meaning, using the syntax, or sounding out words based on phonics rules or prior knowledge of words with similar prefixes, suffixes, or roots (Keene & Zimmerman, 1997)

When teachers select one or a cocktail of these strategies as discussion foci, struggling readers can observe the strategies of good readers when student groups are formed by mixed-ability reading skills. Talking through something aids understanding (Vygotsky, 1978). In reading workshop approaches to discussion, teachers use their own talk to walk themselves out of confusion they face with a textual passage, identify the strategy that supports their access back into comprehension, and then release responsibility for students to use their own strategies as the teacher nudges them into comprehension by asking "uptake questions" (follow-up questions) to guide students to a deeper level of thinking about a passage (McIntyre, 2007). A selected strategy can be an emphasis for a discussion with students documenting the number of times a strategy was used with a difficult passage. Supplying students with copies of difficult passages, having students notate when and where they are stuck with a coding system, and using discussion time to repair comprehension *is* balanced literacy discussion.

Reciprocal Teaching (Palincsar & Brown, 1984) uses four strategies that work well together during textual discussion: predicting, questioning, seeking clarification, and summarizing. Diehl (2005) recommends that students document their thinking with graphic organizers. She recommends that students begin to discuss texts by asking clarifying and wondering questions before, during, and after reading. As they read, students add prediction statements that are justified by passages based on the text and the readers' prior knowledge.

McIntyre (2007) recommends that teachers who want to use discussion as a language tool to develop balanced literacy skills in students create the following scaffolding support. Some of her instruction will sound familiar by now, especially honoring the process of student negotiation of meaning before barging in with the teacher's correct point of view.

- Provide explicit directions for students, including stating the purpose for reading a passage, setting procedures for participating in discussion, and defining the strategy or strategies that work well with the passage.

- Cue students to what they should especially notice in the text by emphasizing a direction ("*Respond* to what Student X just said"); slow down, indicate a word or phrase that might be important, repeat for emphasis.

- Restate a student turn in order for group members to recognize its importance and as an invitation for the student or peers to elaborate.

- Do not evaluate or critique a student turn so as not to derail student talk, but let students know that their contributions were heard by the teacher and appreciated.

- Offer students opportunities to practice group problem solving.

- Over time, as balanced literacy discussion becomes a routine, let students take more and more responsibility in articulating their strategies for figuring out complex texts without teacher cueing.

We appreciate the explicit strategy instruction of balanced literacy, especially for struggling readers, and think that it contributes much to making good reading visible as students think about what text might mean.

Discussion Formats

Several kinds of discussion possibilities are described in recent reading research. Discussions can be organized around read-alouds, can be student led, can rely more heavily on the written word rather than on the spoken word, and can be by the whole class or in small groups.

Discussions Around Read-Alouds

Interactive read-alouds (Barrentine, 1996) is a whole-class discussion format that focuses on meaning-making as the teacher reads a text orally to a class. Students are asked to spontaneously add to the conversation, especially their aesthetic responses, and explain to peers how they are making sense of a passage using balanced literacy strategies. Several kinds of student initiations have been identified (Maloch & Beutel, 2010, p. 23) and can be tallied by teachers as discussion ensues to see the strengths and weaknesses of student comprehension during discussion:

- Connections made to personal experience, other texts, the world, future experiences, shared experiences
- Predictions of what will happen next in the text
- Clarifying vocabulary, details, storyline, or truth-value of passages in literature
- Observing the text or illustrations closely and making meaning from multimodal forms of text
- Entering the story world by relating to characters, making comments about their actions, and suggesting changes students would make if they wrote the text
- Offering directions about process such as how the teacher should direct the activity

Maloch observes that interactive read-alouds, like all rich discussion, require a low-risk environment in which students' assertions about texts are invited and validated by the teacher. Teachers take care to revoice student contributions, especially those of reticent students, and redirect student questions and assertions back to peers.

Student-Led Discussions

Student-led discussions (Morocco & Hindin, 2002) are composed of groups of four or five students who gather shared interpretations of a text. Teachers first describe to the class peer discussion roles—which can be determined by assigning a literacy strategy to each group member or a functional role such as timekeeper, director, recorder, or presenter—and explain what the role entails. Teachers must then proscribe rules for discussion norms (do not interrupt, maintain good eye contact, etc.). Students take on their specific roles and interpret a text together. Morocco and Hindin describe several ways that students might work together to form these interpretations (p. 151). The explicit reasoning of argumentation should be described to students with examples across texts. A discussion around an argument consists of the following discourse moves that work better when documented with student writing.

- The student makes an interpretive claim about a passage.
- Group members elaborate on that interpretation.

- An alternative claim about the same passage is offered by a group member.

- Group members can question assumptions of claims using close reading and citing textual evidence.

- Claims should be revised or synthesized as students consider counterclaims that make more sense.

- Consider counterclaims and arguments for validity.

- Request precise wording of an argument.

- Test alternative claims.

- Consider a character's personal/social world, especially through identification with the character or making text-to-self connections.

- Engage in hypothetical reasoning about characters' choices and consequences of those choices.

- Apply interpretations to group experiences.

- Summarize group thinking for assessment data of reading comprehension.

Students can prepare arguments regarding a passage before being grouped in a discussion in which they make an assertion about the passage and offer textual evidence to support their claim.

Written Discussions

Written discussions, also called dialogue journals or partner journals, are yet another way to discuss important themes in literature. Harvey and Bizar (1998) outline how students can ponder important passages in texts after reading. Students are assigned to pairs and write short notes to each other about important passages (the teacher can select these or have students pick passages that resonated with them personally). Simultaneously, students write notes to one another (perhaps they can text if they have cell phones on their persons) in response to agreed upon reading selections. Every two or three minutes, when notified by the teacher, they exchange notes. This is done three or four times while students remain quiet. The first time, a note is written in reaction to a passage. Previous messages piggyback on previous responses to the partner. Teachers can direct students to particular kinds of responses ("What did you wonder about in this passage?" or "Did you agree with this character's decision in that passage?"). After the designated exchanges, students can talk aloud about their responses with their partners. If and when conversations move to a whole-class discussion, students are more likely to have something of greater value to share.

Whole-class discussions are more likely to be generative if the teacher has scaffolded them through small-group discussions in which students realize they have substantive contributions to make. Gritter (2010) recommends the following strategies for scaffolding whole-class discussions:

- Shy students are more likely to share what they really think about literature if they are grouped with friends (Hartup, 1996). Reading journal entries (or the entries of friends) is another, "safer" way to share a response to a literary passage with a whole class.

- The rules for talking about text need to be shared. Students should be seated to address each other and not just the teacher. Eye contact and body language send signals of active listening, as does quoting what other students have said before agreeing or disagreeing with other students or the teacher. Teachers should tell students that they are going to be acting as facilitators and will deliberately try to not dominate textual talk.

- Let students know how and when their discussion will be assessed.

- Inform students of new classroom management routines more suitable for livelier discussion. Raising hands can act as a dam against the flow of speech. A speaking stick or "hot seat" chairs for speakers may be an alternative way to manage talk.

- Disagreement is fine if it is defended with examples from one's experience or textual matter. Students should know that disagreement is important to a functioning democracy.

- Students must be taught to ask layered questions of text. They should ask literal questions of text when they are confused, inferential questions where they read between the lines of text, and critical questions that get to the heart of social justice in terms of textual matter.

- Layers of questions, especially inferential and critical questions, can be flipped into assertions and documented as new learning.

Whatever the format of textual discussion (and often one format leads into another), students should be able to articulate that they have considered new points of view and be able to ultimately argue with their final assertions about the meaning of text.

Social Identities Matter!

For current secondary students, literacy practices (reading, writing, discussing/communicating, listening) are socially situated, located in a particular time, place, and space, and shaped by the popular culture that surrounds them (film, the Internet, social media, popular music). Scholars like Barton, Hamilton, and Ivanic (2000) write:

> All uses of . . . language can be seen as located in particular times and places. . . . One result of the focus on literacy as a social practice is that literacies are positioned in relation to the social institutions and power relations which sustain them. (p. 1)

For 21st century students, popular texts are part of the social institutions that frame and shape literacy and social practice. Hagood, Alvermann, and Heron-Hruby (2010) write:

> [Connecting] pop culture texts, school texts, and texts students create . . . develop[s] the necessary competencies for 21st-century demands. Connecting texts that blur across contexts addresses the educational purposes of acknowledging and building on students' literacies in order to enable them to learn both relevant content and the thinking process that can lead to productive and fulfilled lives. (p. 2)

Texts from popular culture position the literacy practices of today's students. Literature discussions (using popular texts) acknowledge and reveal this positioning. In this way, what the students already know is recognized. An additional result of using popular texts in literature discussions is that as students hear the connections their peers are making based on other (popular) cultural experiences and understandings, they learn from what their peers know.

Discussions can be socially loaded literacy events. Language, including language that references popular culture, can be a tool that brands "right" and "wrong" sorts of people, particularly for adolescents who are trying to figure out who they are in terms of their social surroundings. Bucholtz and Hall (2005) observe that instead of being an internal and fixed psychological state, identity emerges in cultural and social interactions using language. Identities become linguistically indexed in language encounters as speakers and listeners label each other based on perceptions of language ability. The indexing of language process enables speakers and listeners to form identities based on relationships with each other. These identities can be intentional and unintentional.

A current lens for understanding the adolescent mind places language and literacy as a nexus for adolescent development and identity formation. This lens, termed *youth culture*, places adolescents within a sociocultural context that posits that language is social as well as linguistic (McCarthey & Moje, 2002). Who is talking might matter to a discussion group as much or more than what is being said. Because language is social, it can serve as an "identity kit" to reveal adolescent development (Gee, 1996). Youth culture theories emphasize the subjective, context-specific nature of how adolescents view themselves and operate in a group dynamic. Hawkins (2004) observes that "each language is composed of many different 'social languages,' that is, different styles of languages that communicate different socially-situated identities (who is acting) and socially-situated identities that are integrally connected to social groups, cultures, and historical formations" (p. 3). Gee notes that utterances occurring in social languages serve two interrelated purposes: to make the speaker come off as a particular kind of person and to come off as a person engaged in a particular socially situated activity (p. 13). Class discussions can be fora of great uncertainty for adolescents because they are navigating a tightrope of what they actually think about text and how peers and teachers may be labeling them as they articulate their ideas in public spaces. Worthham (2004) calls this anxiety "social identification"—the process by which individuals and groups are marked as belonging to particular collectivities or demographics. Within the broad spectrum of adolescent culture, social categories of individuals are in place in classrooms, and individuals must display characteristics that fit into these categories if they want to be seen as members of a particular identity group.

Rich literature discussion does not happen without the formation of a safe literary community. In practice, dialogic and permeable textual discussion looks a lot like group therapy. Yalom (1995), a therapist, offers some norms for therapists who seek high peer interaction during group therapy. These are valuable for literature teachers as well. Good discussion happens in environments where expression is honest and spontaneous. This means that traditional classroom management practices such as requiring students to raise their hands before speaking will probably get in the way of spontaneous speech. Good discussion also requires that class members be free to have honest interactions, especially as they are referencing their own lives, cultures, and ways of thinking. This does not entail that all students be best friends, but classroom members must have some trust in each other if students are expected to share deeply felt emotions and ideas. High peer interaction requires personal involvement in a class. Students must feel some bond with their teacher and classmates, must want insight into literature, and must be willing to change their first reaction to literature based on active listening. Students must also believe they can change their minds and still be true to themselves. Self-disclosure when making connections with literature must be highly valued and feel safe if it is to be common classroom practice (Nystrand, 1997). Needless to say, discussions may not start off great at the beginning of the year. Discussions need to be scaffolded, and students play a large role in their success. Anonymously surveying students about how they *felt* (and why they felt that way) after early discussions is one way teachers can assess whether students are building an atmosphere of trust.

What Is Popular Culture? And Why Does It Matter to ELA Teachers?

The impetus for this book comes, in part, from Kristine's involvement in a presentation at a national conference. The presentation asked the question "Can Hamlet and Lady

Gaga coexist in the ELA classroom?" This presentation was then featured in an online article (http://blog.oregonlive.com). And while the article featuring the presentation was a positive albeit brief overview, the comments that were posted serve to illustrate some of the issues that arise when ELA teachers think about incorporating, or when they do incorporate, texts from popular culture into their classrooms.

While many of the comments left on the website were generally positive regarding the use of popular culture in literature discussions (some even citing the popular texts their own English teachers used), many comments were both negative and critical, revealing a hierarchical stance toward both popular texts and literature. For example, one post reads, "Of course Lady Gaga and Hamlet can coexist in the classroom. All that you need to do is redefine 'culture' and 'art' down to their lowest possible meaning" (http://blog.oregonlive.com).

Another commenter wrote:

The biggest problem is that young people (actually most adults, too) don't understand how to think critically, to actually understand why one position is more logically sound than another[,] or to understand why one piece of art is worthy of praise while another is crap. To put it more plainly, when discussing "The Great Gatsby" [sic] and the song "Gold Digger" one needs to make very clear why one is considered a literary masterpiece and the other is garbage, even though they may make similar points. Unfortunately, this approach has been going on forever and is essentially a cheap, easy short cut to try and get young people to understand why great art is considered great. What happens is that kids start to equate popular culture, which by and large is forgettable refuse, with art that has actual lasting power. Lady Gaga will be [forgotten] in a few years. Robert Frost will not. There is a reason why. That is the kind of thing that must be taught, critical thinking skills. (ibid)

Two things are interesting to note here. First, and most obvious, is the idea that there is a cultural hierarchy in which popular texts (Kanye West's "Gold Digger") get placed at the bottom and artistic texts (F. Scott Fitzgerald's *The Great Gatsby*) get placed at the top (or, as mentioned earlier, Adele lands closer to the top of the hierarchy and Carly Rae Jepsen lands a bit lower, even though both artists enjoyed a "most popular song" status). There seems to be an unspoken, yet somehow strangely obvious, assumption that everyone knows the difference between art, which has "lasting power," and not-art (popular culture), which is "forgettable refuse."

One teacher, in response to the question "Do you consider popular culture as art?" responded, "I hate to say it, but I don't think I do. . . . I think things that are valuable take time to create, and rest on pure emotions and pure messages. . . . [Popular artists] have so much help [today] . . . you can access things so much easier. . . . I feel like there's a lot more help involved today. Things aren't as pure as . . . it doesn't involve as much skill." It's this apparent difference in what is involved in creating art and what is involved in creating popular texts that drives much of the debate about what can be, and should be, included in the ELA classroom. The attitude communicated is that by incorporating popular culture, we are "[redefining] 'culture' and 'art' down to their lowest possible meaning" and we "make very clear why one is considered a literary masterpiece (*The Great Gatsby*) and the other is garbage ("Gold Digger")." The result of this unspoken, yet strangely obvious assumption is the idea that English language arts should be a place and space where only literary masterpieces are studied, leaving popular culture texts—"the garbage"—to be consumed outside of the sacred place and space of the ELA classroom.

An interesting idea to note is that none of the commenters mentioned their own interactions with, or uses of, popular culture. So, while there seemed to be a strangely clear assumption in operation regarding what is and is not considered "art" or "a literary masterpiece," there was not any indication of the fact that popular texts are prevalent and pervasive. So although adults and adolescents, at some level, engage with popular texts, we, particularly ELA teachers, often don't talk about the manner in which we evoke and engage with popular texts as we discuss—or *in the same way* we discuss—literary masterpieces. In fact, one teacher noted:

> But there's the part of me that wants to be the studious English teacher that says, 'I'm a scholar and I'm not going to waste my time on [pop music star/actor] Ashlee Simpson's wedding.' But I bought *People* [a celebrity gossip/human interest magazine] the day it came out because I wanted to see Ashlee Simpson's wedding. So, I realize that it's a paradox, but I don't really know what to do with it. . . . It's [being a "studious" English teacher who consumes popular magazines] so obnoxious of me. (Schoon-Tanis, 2010, p. 120)

It seems, then, that in addition to a type of cultural hierarchy by which we measure texts, we also carry with us a level of discomfort about the texts we regularly consume. If we, as ELA teachers, feel so conflicted about our own personal uses of popular texts, it makes sense, then, that we would feel conflicted about incorporating popular texts into literature discussions.

As mentioned in Chapter 1, a best practice in the ELA classroom is to discuss literature. And part of discussing literature is activating prior knowledge or incorporating shared knowledge. In many cases, for adults as well as for adolescents, using texts from popular culture is a way to activate this prior knowledge. So, while having a discussion about the artistic or aesthetic worth of Kanye West is, we would argue, a necessary and worthwhile conversation, using students' knowledge of, and experience with, West's music to make real-world connections with the required literature of ELA classrooms is even more necessary and worthwhile. Often, however, the problem is that we all, teachers and students alike, operate with an aesthetic hierarchy that goes both unspoken and unexamined. It's this hierarchy that allows us to make statements such as, "Kanye West is garbage," "Lady Gaga is forgettable," and Adele is a "better" artist with more "staying power" than Carly Rae Jepsen. However, we argue that there is, indeed, a place for popular culture texts in ELA both as a catalyst for discussion and as a gateway, or stepping stone, that leads students from what they know (popular texts) to works of literature with which they are unfamiliar and unexperienced. In many ways, using popular texts with the texts of the canon is a way to progress toward more critical and complex thinking.

The truth of the matter is that more and more ELA teachers are using texts from popular culture to activate students' prior knowledge in order to enhance class discussions even if they feel conflicted and uncomfortable with such a move. Because more and more teachers are, indeed, incorporating popular culture into classroom instruction (Cawelti, 2004; Durham & Kellner, 2001; Morrell, 2004; Strinati, 1995), it is important not only to know what the argument is for the inclusion of popular culture, but also to know how popular culture texts are used in conjunction with traditional, canonical texts. That is, it's important to know how secondary ELA teachers are talking about, and defining, the curricular use of popular culture particularly in regard to literature discussion. In order to begin examining the literature, defining or delineating (Guins & Cruz, 2005, p. 17) "popular culture" is a necessary first step to take. And this is where the first rub begins.

Popular Culture

In order to gain understanding of the conversations teachers and scholars have about incorporating popular texts into literature discussions, defining popular culture—in contrast to other terms and ideas that surround theories of popular culture such as mass media[1] or media studies—is an important initial step. However, defining popular culture really means defining both "popular" and "culture" as well as defining "popular culture"—a task that is more complicated than just putting together two definitions of two seemingly contrasting words. As Guins and Cruz (2005) write in the introduction to their edited volume *Popular Culture: A Reader*: "A commonly held view on popular culture is that it is simultaneously incredibly easy to talk about . . . and incredibly difficult to talk about" (p. 3). This introductory comment makes one think about the idea "I know it when I see it."

A somewhat typical, or traditional, definition of popular culture comes from Mahiri (2001), who considers popular culture to be the "modes of transmission (e.g., TV, the Internet, video games, music compact discs, movies) that are capable of presenting a variety of textual forms like print, pictures, drawings, animation, and sound" (p. 382). A similar definition is Strinati's (1995): "The sense of popular culture

I have in mind is indicated by . . . a set of generally available artefacts: films, records, clothes, TV programmes, modes of transport, etc." (p. xvii). While Strinati's definition seems to include and allow for more categories (i.e., transportation), both definitions seem a bit too vague and all-inclusive; these definitions, while focusing on artifacts of modes of communication, do not seem to define what is "popular" about these artifacts, nor do they explain how the artifacts would be considered as elements of "culture." After reading these definitions of popular culture, we assume that popular culture comprises only the artifacts mass-produced by current global technology. We would not necessarily come to a greater understanding of what is meant by "popular culture" through this reading or understanding. Nor would we come to a greater understanding of the potential and possibility for using popular texts in the ELA classroom. More is needed to differentiate between popular culture and other forms of culture, as well as between popular culture and mass media. More is needed to understand the debate and discussion regarding using popular texts in literature discussions. It is important to closely examine how the label "popular culture" is used and understood.

Popular

The place where many scholars begin in delineating "popular culture" is by theorizing the use of the word "popular." Guins and Cruz (2005) write: "The term 'popular' houses a broad range of meanings. Incorporating folk cultures' link to organic community—of the people—as well as mass cultures' status—being well liked or merely widely available—popular culture brings together diverse and sometimes contradictory associations" (p. 9; see also Storey, 2003). Storey (2006) in his initial explanation of popular culture offers a similar description: "An obvious starting point in any attempt to define popular culture is to say that popular culture is simply culture which is widely favoured or well liked by many people" (p. 4). Because of the contradictory associations—that is, the difficulty in distinguishing between "of the people" and "well liked" or "widely available"—the route that many authors take in dealing with this stage of the process, seemingly in order to make the process smoother, is to replace "popular" with "mass." Thus, mass culture (of a large group of people) rather than popular culture (well liked or widely available) becomes the guideline in discussing and describing this particular aspect of culture. Macdonald (1957/2005) in "A Theory of Mass Culture" writes: "It is sometimes called 'Popular Culture,' but I think 'Mass Culture' a more accurate term, since its distinctive mark is that it is solely and directly an article for mass consumption, like chewing gum" (Guins & Cruz, 2005, p. 39). Without acknowledging that chewing gum could be considered popular culture in its own way, by replacing "popular" or "popular culture" with "mass" or "mass culture" in this way shifts the connotation of the label. Specifically, such an exchange

Implies a shift from culture or a piece of culture that is pervasive to culture or a piece of culture that is massively gobbled up like chewing gum.

In a slightly different vein, Williams (1976/2005) summarizes two common understandings of "mass." In his essay defining both "mass" and "culture," he writes:

> In the modern social sense, then, masses and mass have two distinguishable kinds of implication. Masses (i) is the modern word for *many-headed multi-tude* or *mob*: low, ignorant, unstable. Masses (ii) is a description of the same people, but now seen as a positive or potentially positive social force. (2005, p. 31, emphasis in original)

Both Macdonald (1957/2005) and Williams employ "mass" to signify a multitude rather than allowing for the place or role of an element of being well liked or widely accepted. And while Williams does open the door to a mob having the potential for being a positive social force, this positive view is not prevalent in the literature describing mass, or popular, culture. Instead of "popular" connoting someone or something that is well liked by many, "mass" implies a mob mentality of many people moving or consuming herdlike without thinking or feeling; and even if such move-ment is sometimes for a positive purpose, or sometimes for a negative purpose, mass movement signifies a removal of agency. By interchanging the words "popular" and "mass," theorists like Williams and Macdonald change the way this form of culture is understood, often by implying a negative element of mob mentality, a negative con-notation that, unfortunately, often is used to refer to adolescents.

Shiach (1989/2005) in her essay "The Popular" continues to explain and expound on the difficulty in coming to a consensus in terms of delineating the "popular" in popular culture. Shiach, in her historical tracing of the use of "popular," writes:

> All of these examples represent attempts to utilize the apparent universality of ['popular' meaning of] 'the people' while simultaneously demarcating the boundaries of 'the people' in relation to political power. At other moments, however, 'popular' refers quite explicitly to one part of the social formation: those 'of lowly birth; belonging to the commonalty or populace; plebeian.' . . . 'Popular' thus becomes associated with a cluster of themes attributed to those of low social standing. (Guins & Cruz, 2005, p. 57)

Shiach continues on to compare and contrast how the word "popular" has not only been used to demarcate boundaries of people, but also has meant both "of the peo-ple" and "for the people" (Guins & Cruz, 2005, p. 58). In all of her discussion, she demonstrates the difficulty of defining "popular" by elucidating the difficulty of defin-ing the political and/or social positioning of "people," as well as of defining what is "of" or "for" the people. The task to define "popular" is challenging when the task to characterize "people"—a necessary element in discussing "popular"—is just as complicated. Consequently, whether using "popular" or "mass" to describe a particular aspect of culture, scholars have a difficult time characterizing and classifying both "popular" and "people" for the purposes of coming to some understanding about culture. In some ways, it would seem that such difficulty would be refreshing and would lead to interesting conversations.

However, such interesting conversations are made more complicated as many authors, such as Leavis (1930/2005), Benjamin (1936/2001), Adorno and Horkheimer (1944/2001), Macdonald (1957/2005), Nye (1970), and Williams (1976/2005), make use of a negative view of both "the people" and "the masses." That is to say, instead of approaching popular culture as something that is widely available, these scholars approach popular culture as mass consumption. Adorno and Horkheimer write:

> The most intimate reactions of human beings have been so thoroughly reified that the idea of anything specific to themselves now persists only as an utterly abstract notion: personality scarcely signifies anything more than shining white teeth and freedom from body odor and emotions. The triumph of [mass culture] in the culture industry is that consumers feel compelled to buy and use its products even though they see through them. (1944/2001, p. 101)

What these authors communicate is a view of the masses that become the mob that blindly consumes without thought, taste, or conviction, many even going so far as to explicitly ignore their own desires. This is the view that allows comments similar to stating that Kanye West's "Gold Digger" is "garbage." As a result, as the term "popular" shifts to mean "of the masses," the view of popular culture one receives by reading these theorists is a negative view—even though there seems to be little agreement on what "popular" even means.

Culture

Agreeing, or coming to a consensus, on a definition or delineation of "culture" seems to be just as difficult as for "popular": The term "culture" is often used to refer to a wide array of elements in human life. "The very essence of culture," Cawelti (2004) writes,

> lies in the relationship we have with the things we unquestioningly love, enjoy, and choose to involve ourselves in. We sometimes lose sight of this in the attempt to winnow our enthusiasms and order them into patterns that, transcending the pleasure of the moment, can become part of a cultural heritage that is passed on from one generation to another. (p. 121)

Cawelti, then, has a broad view of culture, one that includes any and all of the natural, normal, or ordinary aspects of living. Similarly, Durham and Kellner (2001) write: "Culture is ordinary, a familiar part of every day life" (p. 6), and John Storey (2003) in his book *Inventing Popular Culture* writes: "In very broad terms, culture is how we live in nature . . . it is how we make sense of ourselves and the world around us" (pp. ix–x). According to these theorists, then, culture is an inherent element in everyday living; it is an ordinary part of life that influences how we make sense of ourselves, as well as how we make sense of the world and environments in which we live.

However, not all theorists ascribe to such an all-inclusive view of culture. Williams (1976/2005) explains: "[T]he most widespread use [of "culture"] . . . is music, literature, painting and sculpture, theatre and film" (p. 27). Thus, while some are willing to expand the idea of culture to include all elements of ordinary life and living, according to the definition explicated by Williams, the most widely accepted use of the term is that which describes art and artistic artifacts, thus limiting the term "culture" to only the tangible objects of cultural production—tangible objects that "are saturated with social meanings [and] generate political effects, reproducing or opposing governing social institutions and relations of domination and subordination" (Durham & Kellner, 2001, p. 6). Or, for our purposes, "culture" includes the texts and artifacts of the ELA classroom—the texts and artifacts that are saturated with social meaning. It seems, then, that this is where the idea of "culture" becomes a hierarchical notion, similar to the move of delineating popular culture as mass culture. That is, there are texts that have more social meaning (songs by Adele) than others (songs by Carly Rae Jepsen). Additionally, it seems that this is where the notion of a literary canon originates—tangible objects (print) that "are saturated with . . . meaning" (Arnold's "the best that has been thought and said").

To further the diverse positions regarding the delineation of "culture," in describing a hierarchical view of culture (the texts of the literary canon compared with the texts of popular culture), Guins and Cruz (2005) write: "[The] hierarchy [is] premised upon separations between culture and civilization, the equation of 'culture' with perfections and goodness, and social progress/order (cultural preservation) through education" (p. 5). Hence, in addition to the artifacts of culture, Guins and Cruz add that the use of the term "culture" also implies a standard of goodness or order that can be passed on, or maintained, only through education. And, it seems, the assumption is that this cultural education will happen in ELA through the transmission of the literary canon. This conceptualization of culture began with Matthew Arnold's work in 1932, when "the word 'culture' acquired a more restrictive meaning . . . referring now to a state of intellectual refinement associated with the arts, philosophy and learning" (duGay et al., 1997, p. 11). As a result, the notion of "culture" for many theorists includes the good or perfect cultural artifacts created and preserved through a particular (often, "elite") education. That is, culture, for these theorists, is not part of the everyday but is a specific, highly valued, admired aspect of life able to be passed on only through the transmission of (English) education. Cawelti (2004) touches on this tension between culture as ordinary and culture as good and perfect when he writes:

> Normatively, the concept of culture was a unifying ideal, centered on a vision of Western civilization as the climax of cultural progress and synthesis. This vision inspired the idea of the humanistic curriculum as pedagogy, leading the student to acquire a significant proportion of the artistic and philosophical canon thought to define this civilization. On the other hand, used descriptively by the late nineteenth-century disciplines of anthropology, sociology, and social psychology, culture was a concept that articulated the multiplicity of behaviors characteristic of actual human beings in different places and times. . . . Growing doubts about the value or even the possibility of a unified culture have increasingly led critics and scholars to use the word 'culture' with qualifying adjectives—popular, working class, ethnic, folk, high, low, and middle, global, etc. The word of the postmodern is no longer culture but *hyphen-culture*. (pp. 252–53, emphasis added)

In order to reach some sort of delineation of the term "culture," many scholars and theorists have resorted to qualifying or describing these "hyphen-cultures," or what some call "subcultures," and through such description have relegated certain artifacts or discourses of culture to a more prestigious level and esteemed label than others (thus, a cultural hierarchy). What a number of scholars in the social sciences have offered to the discussion about culture is a view of culture that is more common and everyday; however, by labeling and qualifying (in using adjectives to describe it), the concept of culture becomes only more confusing and convoluted. Instead of expounding or explaining, such labels prohibit and perplex, as well as devalue and diminish. Culture of the ordinary and everyday becomes culture of particular categories, and those categories are then placed along a cultural hierarchy; and the idea of ELA transmitting a "higher" culture becomes even more entrenched. While some ideas from the social sciences offered a new and more holistic view of culture according to Cawelti (2004), these ideas only served to further differentiate and stratify. Even though some scholars who study culture and popular culture maintain an all-inclusive, ordinary definition of culture, many theorists still maintain a position of culture that labels and excludes based on a supposed hierarchy of art and artistic artifacts—a view that gets passed down to ELA classrooms.

However, Durham and Kellner (2001) offer a different take on the hierarchical debate when they write: "We . . . employ the term 'culture' broadly to signify types of cultural artifacts (i.e., TV, CDs, newspapers, paintings, opera, journalism, cyberculture, and so on), as well as discourses about these phenomena. Since culture is bound up in both *forms* . . . and *discourses*, it is both a space of interpretation and debate as well as subject matter and domain of inquiry" (p. 3, emphasis added). What these authors offer is a way to think and talk about culture from a number of angles and perspectives, including both the artifacts of culture and the idea of culture as ordinary life and living. Or, as Hagood and colleagues (2010) write: "[I]t is . . . crucial to understand how texts function as social practices that show identities, values, beliefs, and social networks" (p. 3). By contributing a way to talk about both the artifacts of culture in addition to the ordinariness of life as culture and conversations that happen around culture, Durham and Kellner present an opportunity to change, or to start a new dialogue about, culture. As such, they do not imply a strict differentiation within culture or between subcultures or Cawelti's (2004) "hyphen-cultures." Instead of viewing popular culture as a parasite on elite culture or as chewing gum (Macdonald, 1957/2005), Durham and Kellner, through their "different take" on culture, offer a way to talk about the myriad elements that influence and inform culture. This, then, is what Storey (1996) refers to when he writes that "culture [is not] defined in the narrow sense, as the objects of aesthetic excellence ('high art'); nor [is it] defined in an equally narrow sense as a process of aesthetic, intellectual and spiritual development; but [it is] understood as the texts and practices of everyday life" (p. 2); that is, for some theorists, culture is both the forms *and* discourses of culture.

Popular Culture in ELA

Even though many scholars and theorists cannot seem to come to a common conclusion regarding the definition and delineation of either "popular" or "culture," or of popular culture's place in contemporary society, the use of popular culture in the secondary ELA classroom continues and is encouraged to continue. And while many theorists have a negative view of popular culture either because it is seen as a threat to (elite) cultural standards or because it is seen as manipulative of the masses (Storey, 2003, p. 30), many ELA teachers have a positive view of popular culture in that they see the use of popular texts as a manner of allowing them to help students gain access to literature (in addition to allowing them to try to bridge the gap between home and school literacies, as well as allowing them to incorporate diversity into the classroom). Renee Hobbs (1998) in "Literacy for the Information Age" writes: "[E]ducators are coming to recognize that literacy is not simply a matter of acquiring decontextualized decoding, comprehension, and production skills, but that the concept of literacy must be connected with the culture and contexts in which reading and writing are used" (n.p.). Likewise, Ernest Morrell (2004) writes: "The alleged literacy crisis in today's schools is not so much a testament to regressing classroom instruction and student achievement as it is a testament to the increasing literacy demands of a postindustrial, techno-literate society" (p. 3). Connecting literacy with the context of students' lived experiences spurs a number of teachers to include popular culture texts in the ELA classroom. The disagreement about what qualifies as popular culture, or not, does not deter a number of teachers from using popular texts in order to enhance rich literature discussions.

While not all teachers agree, some teachers see the use of popular culture in conjunction with traditional canonical texts as a way to discuss and connect the social and cultural context of textual consumption and production; they see using popular culture in the classroom as a way to bridge the gaps between students' home and school literacies. Hobbs (1998) writes, "Many teachers are increasingly using mass media 'texts' to enrich their subject . . . comfortably moving between the textbook, the trade book, the newspaper, the film and the videotape in their efforts to bring rich ideas into the classroom" (n.p.). Thus, even though the debate about the definition, role, and place of popular culture in current society and education continues, secondary ELA teachers maintain and increase the use of popular culture in their classrooms in a variety of ways, and for a variety of reasons, in connection with literacy. This book explores and examines how teachers can enact these practices for the purpose of augmenting students' experiences with literature and for the purpose of enhancing and enriching discussion of literature.

Opportunity for Reflection

Consider how you might apply the ideas from this chapter to your own classroom.

1. What do you think about Ms. P's rules for discussion? Would they work with your own students?

2. Describe some alternative or additional rules for student participation you could use in your own classroom.

3. How might you track student participation?

4. Which discussion formats have you tried? Which do you want to try more? Why or why not?

5. How would you define pop culture?

Note

1. Kathryn was in her middle years of graduate school when she finally realized that "media" meant forms of communication and "mass media" was a term indicating the forms of media used to reach the largest audience. It was only then that she stopped using both "media" and "mass media" interchangeably to refer to film, television, news media (both print and televised), popular magazines, advertisements, and popular music and started using "popular culture" instead.

3 Literary Discussion and the Common Core State Standards

As we write this chapter, most states have determined learning targets for what American students will be learning in their English language arts classrooms. The new learning targets are called the Common Core State Standards, and, as they are new, they are making teachers and principals nervous because they are generally considered to be more rigorous than the standards they are replacing.

The good news, we think, is that discussion is an important part of many anchor standards.

The Common Core State Standards require that students read complex texts that, over time and across the grades, adequately prepare them for college. The Common Core standards mandate that teachers explicitly teach genre components when teaching literature and connect literary genres with student writing tasks. As students engage in literacy, they are to work together and actively listen to each other as they learn to integrate information from oral, visual, quantitative, and media sources. As we will show in future chapters, literary discussion referencing popular culture can help students meet Common Core standards. Finally, students are also to make decisions on language (standard English or informal language) based on audience and purpose when presenting to a group.

As we peruse the Common Core standards (we chose seventh-grade anchor standards for reading literature and speaking and listening as examples), we see that discussion is an appropriate instructional tool for students to master *all* of the anchor standards in literary reading and for speaking and listening. Consider the following tasks required of seventh-grade students in the anchor standards for reading literature (designated as RL followed by the number 7 for seventh grade, then the number of the standard):

- Cite textual evidence to support claims (RL.7.1)
- Cite textual evidence to support inferences drawn from text as students read between the lines of text (RL.7.1)

- State the theme of a text (RL.7.2)

- Analyze how a text plot develops (RL.7.2)

- Summarize a text (RL.7.2)

- Analyze how aspects of story grammar (characters, setting, dialogue, conflict, resolution) create cause and effect (RL.7.2)

- Unpack the meaning of unknown words, figurative expressions, and inferences of words (RL.7.4)

- Analyze how rhyme and poetic play with words affect the meaning and pleasurable reading of literature (RL.7.4, RL.7.5)

- Compare and contrast points of view of characters in a text (RL.7.6)

- Compare written literature to film, play, and multimedia by analyzing similarities and differences in artistic techniques across media (RL.7.7)

- Compare and contrast fictional accounts with historical accounts set in the same time period to determine how authors of fiction use or alter history (RL.7.9)

- Read and comprehend literature at grade level complexity (RL.7.10)

Now consider the anchor standards for speaking and listening (SL), giving particular descriptions of what quality discussion should look like in the seventh grade:

- Engage in collaborative discussions in pairs, in small groups, and in teacher-led whole-class discussions with diverse partners with grade level texts, building on the ideas of others and coherently expressing ideas (SL.7.1)

- Research your contributions to discussion (SL.7.1)

- Refer to evidence to support your claims (SL.7.1)

- Probe others to encourage richer discussion so they can reflect on text (SL.7.1)

- Follow rules for liberal discourse where everyone can contribute and defend their opinions (SL.7.1)

- Set goals and roles for discussions and track progress to ensure those goals have been met and roles were completed by group members (SL.7.1)

- Ask questions where group members need to elaborate on their views and respond to others' questions (SL.7.1)

- Bring discussion back to topic when needed (SL.7.1)

- Modify your opinions about text when others share information that helps you to change your mind (SL.7.1)

- Analyze the main ideas and supporting details of messages of diverse media and formats (SL.7.2)

- Explain how ideas clarify a topic or text (SL.7.2)

- Unpack arguments and claims, evaluating the soundness of reasoning and evidence (SL.7.3)

- Present claims and findings in a focused, coherent manner (SL.7.4)

- Demonstrate appropriate eye contact, volume, and pronunciation (SL.7.4)

- Use multimedia components and visual aids to clarify claims and emphasize important points (SL.7.5)

- Adapt speech to formal English when appropriate (SL.7.6)

It is a good idea for teachers to have their learning targets in front of them when planning for a unit. Matt's lesson plans (presented in the next chapter) correlate with the Common Core standards for this unit. Speaking and listening standards for grade 7 are meant to be interconnected with the standards for reading literature.

Before looking at what happened in Matt's class during discussion, it is helpful to look at his learning targets for this unit to show that much of the discussion in Matt's unit is in keeping with present knowledge of optimal learning in language arts classrooms. The actual wording for the speaking and listening grade 7 Common Core standards are in boldface.

- **SL.7.1. Engage effectively in a range of collaborative discussions (one-on-one, in groups, and teacher-led) with diverse partners on grade 7 topics, texts, and issues, building on others' ideas and expressing their own clearly**. During this unit, Matt uses a variety of discussion formats and group settings so that even shy students can demonstrate that they can express their ideas about literature and build on the conversational turns of others.

- **Come to discussions prepared, having read or researched material under study; explicitly draw on that preparation by referring to evidence on the topic, text, or issue to probe and reflect on ideas under discussion.** Matt expects students to complete small chunks of reading for homework and to annotate their books using Post-it Notes. Students are to refer to page numbers and specific passages during some discussions about text. When students do not buttress their claims about text by citing textual passages, he encourages them to do so. When students lead textual discussions, they learn to cue other students to offer textual evidence to support claims. These moves are to become a habit of mind for students. Claims need to be supported.

- **Follow rules for collegial discussions, track progress toward specific goals and deadlines, and define individual roles as needed.** Each Thursday of the four-week unit, small groups of students are responsible for leading a themed whole-class discussion. They must spend significant time defining individual roles and deciding on deep, open-ended questions from text. Examples of planning and implementing student-led discussions will be offered throughout this chapter.

- **Pose questions that elicit elaboration and respond to others' questions and comments with relevant observations and ideas that bring the discussion back on topic as needed.** When students are to lead whole-class discussions, they are to keep discussions on track. When students initiate generative conversational turns that express revelation about a text, discussion leaders are encouraged to follow the train of thought with improvisational finesse. It is impossible to script classroom talk completely.

- **Acknowledge new information expressed by others and, when warranted, modify their own views.** The point of discussion is to create or cement particular interpretations of text with the ultimate learning goal of acquiring new learning because of the insights of others. Students are to exhibit respect for the contributions of all students, even when their conversational turns are at odds with their current thinking. If an unpopular view is expressed, students should ask themselves if they agree or disagree and should feel comfortable supporting an opinion when they have additional evidence to bring to the group.

- **SL.7.2. Analyze the main ideas and supporting details presented in diverse media and formats (e.g., visually, quantitatively, orally) and explain how the ideas clarify a topic, text, or issue under study.** Matt uses audiovisual media as hooks to investigate themes of literature as well as the components or elements of literature that allow students to make sense of themes. Students use themes across diverse media to make claims about art and to buttress their claims with supporting details across those media.

- **SL.7.3. Delineate a speaker's argument and specific claims, evaluating the soundness of the reasoning and the relevance and sufficiency of the evidence.** Ultimately, the point of discussion is to argue for a position that makes the most sense to an individual student: Matt wants students to make reasoned conclusions after examining multiple claims. Students should eventually select claims with the most valid reasoning. A student argument is "warranted" when reasoning aligns with a claim. A student argument is "unwarranted" when the claim cannot be backed by details, examples, or facts. Students need to know the parts of an argument: a claim, evidence leading to warrants, rebuttals to counterclaims, and conclusions. They should use these terms when making arguments about texts in speaking and writing. When students can argue in discussion, they can carry these skills into their writing, but the process of argumentation should be explicitly introduced to students.

- **SL.7.4. Present claims and findings, emphasizing salient points in a focused, coherent manner with pertinent descriptions, facts, details, and examples; use appropriate eye contact, adequate volume, and clear pronunciation.** Public speaking skills are an important part of rich discussion, and all students are to do some public speaking as part of their group presentation. Shy students are not exempt from participating in discussions. Speaking up is necessary for participation in democracy. Dissenting views should be heard and respected, especially if they are logically presented. Students can read from outlines when leading discussions if it helps them keep to pertinent topics of discussion. Students should look at other students when presenting and not just the teacher. Classroom seating should be arranged so that students are able to address each other and not just the teacher. Teachers should be seated among students during discussions and only speak when they need to keep an argument on track.

- **SL.7.5. Include multimedia components and visual displays in presentations to clarify claims and findings and emphasize salient points.** As students present their group discussions, they are to find visual or auditory hooks to keep students engaged in the discussion and for elaboration of main points of the discussion. It is a life skill to put oneself in the shoes of one's listeners. Students must think about activities and discussion topics that will keep their audience engaged. Multimedia sources can help clarify claims made during discussion or examples of important points.

- **SL.7.6. Adapt speech to a variety of contexts and tasks, demonstrating command of formal English when indicated or appropriate.** Public speaking and formal writing during this unit is to be in standard English. However, during discussion, leaders are not to correct the grammar of peers. If students are able to have a whole-class discussion without raising their hands, group leaders can decide that this is acceptable. Leaders can choose to pass a speaking stick around a circle or semicircle or can choose to offer each student different-color "flags" (these can be different colors of paper) to open a new topic of discussion, to agree with another student, to disagree with another student, or to return to a previous topic to add more information.

The following standards deal with reading literature in seventh grade.

- **RL.7.1. Cite several pieces of textual evidence to support analysis of what the text says explicitly as well as inferences drawn from the text.** Note how well this standard works with SL.7.1. Students are to return to the book again and again to justify their responses. A central imperative in Matt's class is that students are not randomly talking about feel-good topics but are enacting the kind of critical textual discussion that is honored in college and in the workplace as civil but substantiated discourse.

- **RL.7.2. Determine a theme or central idea of a text and analyze its development over the course of the text; provide an objective summary of the text.** The discussion groups Matt forms help students explicitly identify themes. Discussions prove that students can summarize texts as they refer to significant events to justify their answers. They show their ability to discuss themes the last day of the unit when the book has been read in its entirety.

- **RL.7.3. Analyze how particular elements of a story or drama interact (e.g., how the setting shapes the characters or plot).** Students are cued to use the literary terms for elements of story grammar (characters, setting, mood, theme, plot, resolution) during their discussions. It is often interesting to discuss how variables in a text work together. Sometimes the personality of a main character makes the plot viable. Sometimes the setting (e.g., a creaky house on a dark and stormy night) becomes a kind of character in a work of literature.

- **RL.7.4. Determine the meaning of words and phrases as they are used in a text, including figurative and connotative meanings; analyze the impact of rhymes and other repetitions of sounds (e.g., alliteration) on a specific verse or stanza of a poem or section of a story or drama.** Although Matt's primary focus is not on the teaching of vocabulary, thematically important words as associated with characters are displayed on walls. In addition, a few conceptually important words are emphasized in each chapter. Students discuss the denotations (dictionary definitions) and connotations (their associations with students) in small groups and are quizzed on these words. Students enjoy using these words in discussion to prove they truly understand sophisticated vocabulary. When listeners hear vocabulary words used in authentic discussion, they notice them and offer kudos to eloquent speakers.

- **RL.7.5. Analyze how a drama's or poem's form or structure (e.g., soliloquy, sonnet) contributes to its meaning**. Students discuss how *A Wrinkle in Time* is a blurred genre of fantasy and science fiction. Television shows and movies are particularly helpful in helping students understand the differences between the two genres.

- **RL.7.6. Analyze how an author develops and contrasts the points of view of different characters or narrators in a text.** As students read the first few chapters, they post pictures of themselves next to the character that seems the most like them. As characters become more rounded through reading and discussion, students can repost their pictures next to different characters.

The Point of Discussions

The reason we are writing this book is not just to help teachers meet the standards but because we think discussions are a key part of studying literature. Discussions demonstrate to diverse learners that they may already have deep connections with the themes and characters of literature. Sometimes all members of the class can have access to the same connections, demonstrating universals of the human experience. Sometimes members of the class have access to different connections, showcasing how cultural values and experiences shape our interpretations of literature. Over time discussions can build classroom communities in which members realize that others value their insights and that classroom members, beyond the teacher, have additional insights into literary texts. Discussions demonstrate that literature offers scripts of situated wisdom from the world in which we live. Plus, from teachers' perspectives, we find that discussions keep previously taught literature fresh and new. Interpretations of literature vary with shifting student populations, and that can be terribly exciting.

As we noted before, discussions are also a best literacy practice. English language arts classrooms in which teachers usually talk and students usually listen do not work for most secondary students who are not intrinsically motivated to study canonical literature. The "teacher talks and I listen" paradigm is an unsound practice for preparing students to become leaders and citizens who participate in democracy. What *does* work is showing students how to systematically argue points of view about text by referencing their text-to-self, text-to-world, and text-to-text connections. Rich discussion might touch on literal comprehension of text but far surpasses knowledge of "just text" to encourage reasoning about text as students actively wrestle with the words of an author and whether what the author has to say is valid from the students' points of view (Langer, 2001). When students who struggle with reading can talk about a text that means something to them, they can enjoy literature, build interpretive skills, find motivation to read more, and talk about social concerns that might not otherwise be discussed (Morocco & Hindin, 2002). Of course, this depends on whether or not an English language arts teacher selects good literature in which characters encounter authentic dilemmas to which students can relate.

Effective discussion results when students learn to argue well and to make connections to what they already know about the world. To learn anything, one must already know something, and teachers who scaffold rich discussions honor what students already know. Textual discussion can be a conduit for several kinds of learning: literary learning as students build interpretations of literature, social understanding of how groups work, and ability to build and maintain an argument by making interpretive claims of a text using comprehension strategies, supporting claims using the words of the text, adding to claims based on the conversational turns of group members, refining claims based on contradictions of other group members, and referencing experiential knowledge to further support claims (Morocco & Hindin, 2002).

Literary discussions are fertile places for students to demonstrate reading comprehension. Maren Aukerman (2008) observes that teachers have three paradigms

41

of reading comprehension that can shape literary discussion: comprehension as an outcome of reading instruction, comprehension as a procedure of reading instruction, and comprehension as sense-making of text. The reading teacher who thinks that discussion should lead to comprehension as an outcome of reading instruction is something of a New Critic. He or she believes that students should find correct answers to predetermined questions as they read and discuss text. The point of a literary discussion for the comprehension-as-outcome teacher is the learning of discrete facts by students as the result of reading and discussing texts. Emphasis is on the texts and not on the readers. This theoretical underpinning does not work with ideals we have for literature discussion.

Teachers who espouse comprehension-as-procedure believe that students should use their reading strategies to find the right answer to confusing portions of text. These teachers have a combination of New Criticism and explicit skills instruction pedagogy. Emphasis is on the procedures leading to right answers, or the fix-it strategies that guide correct understanding of text. We think that discussion in which students have created envisionment with text by applying and voicing the fix-it strategies that allowed them to make sense of textual passages can greatly benefit students who are on the outside looking in. But this paradigm does not totally work with our ideals either.

Aukerman argues, and we agree, that the third paradigm, comprehension as sense-making, is the best model for understanding what students do as they engage in literary discussion and come to understandings of literature. Noting that students make textual hypotheses for social purposes beyond trying to find correct responses, teachers endorsing comprehension as sense-making believe that discussions are both interpersonal and intrapersonal. Discussions demand negotiations among group members and negotiations within a group member's mind as various assertions are explored and ranked, especially if disagreements emerge during textual interpretation. Determining whether or not a group member is saying something that is textually correct is less important than making discoveries about text in the presence of others. Everyone in the group should make discoveries about the text that change over time, becoming better reasoned as discussion ensues. Aukerman proposes that teachers take the following steps to encourage comprehension as sense-making during textual discussion. She calls this process *shared evaluation pedagogy*, or SHEP (Aukerman, 2008).

- Follow student ideas by asking students follow-up questions to clarify the contributions they are trying to make. Understanding what group members are trying to say is critical to examining whether discoveries about text are becoming better reasoned over time. This process can be documented in student writing and can be used as valuable assessment data.

- Articulate textual decision making by asking students to explain how they arrived at conclusions. They should state their textual evidence and their prior knowledge that led them to their conclusions. This process can also be documented in student writing and can be used as valuable assessment data.

- Articulate puzzling or problematic passages or areas where students have disagreements. It is alright for students to have disagreements but they must handle these in well-reasoned ways. We will make conflict negotiation more explicit later in this chapter.

- Hospitably invite quieter group members into the discussion. Teachers should train students to invite all students into a discussion to piggyback on the generative contributions of other students.

- Teachers should actively listen to students. They should allow students to respond to each other first before barging into the conversation.

- Teachers should not hastily evaluate student responses and should encourage students to not rush to judge other students' responses without hearing their evidence first. (pp. 57–8)

These student-centered, response-centered, and argument-driven rules for discussion can bear rich fruit, as we will demonstrate in future chapters. But first we would like to introduce you to a teacher who knows a lot about planning and implementing textual discussions.

Introducing Matt: Middle School Language Arts Teacher

Matt teaches at a private middle school in the Pacific Northwest. He facilitates literature discussions in which students connect classroom literary texts to popular culture as a common instructional practice. In this section, Matt describes why discussions have become a central part of his instructional practices.

Matt's Rationale for Using Discussion as a Teaching Tool

The way young people learn today is very different than the way their parents learned. Classrooms today look different than they used to, visual symbols of changing times and changing learners. The parents of my students grew up in classrooms with textbooks, paperbacks, and pens with notebook paper. Students today have a computer or a tablet to take the place of all three. My students take in information in smaller doses than I did, and that information needs to be high energy and high relevance. My students prefer to interact with the information and connect it to their own personal experience. Perhaps most importantly, they like to interact and connect with their peers. This holds true in the language arts classroom. My students certainly *can* read a book, comprehend the plot, and analyze it on their own, but they get much more out of the book when they have the opportunity to connect with it and to talk about it with their peers.

This year, more than ever, I have noticed the value of peer interaction and discussion about reading. My seventh graders are very bright and very enthusiastic, but they are tough to motivate. When I give an assignment (reading or otherwise) that requires quiet, individual work, I can feel the enthusiasm leave the room. They don't resist the assignments, and they don't do poorly, but they don't "get into it." As a result, they tend not to retain information as well. They see it as busy work, or just an assignment to get in for a grade. This is not to say that I've abandoned those activities or that I've given up on teaching them the importance of individual work. Instead, I have tried to come up with ways to attach discussion and interaction to those activities.

For the first time since I started teaching at this school, I started off the year with book groups. My goal was to have students reading early and often in the school year and to diagnose reading ability and learning styles. I used a selection of seven different books, none of which were overly challenging to read, and all of which featured identifiable characters and plotlines. The only criterion I used for making groups was that no student could read a book that he/she had already read.

I saw very quickly how verbal and experiential my current group of seventh graders was. Since the books were not overly difficult, most students easily kept up with the reading and read with a high level of comprehension. Discussion is where the students really excelled. Each group discussion began with a couple of minutes strictly about the plot and other story elements. After that, the group leader led a discussion that had to be connected to an issue or topic of interest that arose in that section of the book. The leader briefly connected the topic to the story, and then the group talked exclusively about the topic (and not the story). These discussions were fantastic. Students were eager to share personal experiences and opinions. Since they weren't "just talking about the book," the conversations took interesting twists and turns that were relevant and exciting to the students. At the end of the discussion, the group had to tie the discussion back to the book.

After those book groups, I knew that these students needed interaction with each other. They read the books willingly, even though several admitted after the groups that the books weren't their favorites. They also "got something" out of the books and the group discussions. They learned and practiced the unit content, and their critical thinking skills got a workout.

As often as possible this year, I have added discussion and interaction to assignments. Even on simple grammar exercises, I will have students help each other or discuss answers with each other before moving forward. Even when the students are discussing content, it is remarkable how much more engaged they are when they get to talk about their work.

Since those book groups, we have read short stories, novels, and poetry, and small-group discussion has been a key piece of those units. I have found it to be an invaluable tool for learning. It helps students to comprehend what they read because peers can discuss and correct plot details. They learn how to find themes in literature in order to plan and facilitate a discussion about those themes. They learn how to analyze a text and think critically about the characters, the plot, and the themes because they are not simply reading to understand the story. They are reading to make connections.

I can see why a teacher might not be eager to use a great deal of discussion while teaching literature. I have to give up a certain amount of peace and control to do so. Discussions are, at times, rowdy and spirited because middle schoolers are passionate about their interests. Discussions are also difficult to control and plan for. Students can be unpredictable, and they can take discussions into directions that might be difficult to connect to learning. It is certainly more lesson-plan friendly to keep student-led discussions to a minimum.

Intentionally using discussion as a key method for teaching literature has required a change of approach for me. I have always had class discussions, but I have never been as deliberate as I have been this year. I have had to learn how to make discussion and interaction meaningful. I have had to learn how to involve reluctant students. In planning units and lessons, I have had to move away from some of the individual assignments and class work that I have used in the past. That has made it more difficult at times to give individualized reading instruction. It has also required a bit more planning. Coming up with good, meaningful discussion ideas, starters, and questions takes some time. I have to try to keep everyone involved in the discussions and then connect the discussions back to classroom curriculum and skills. Still, it's time well spent because it leads to willing, better readers.

In the next chapters you will see the fruits of Matt's labors. The textual talk of his students shows that a lot of learning is going on. The inclusion of popular culture seems to scaffold this learning.

Opportunity for Reflection

Consider how you might apply the ideas from this chapter to your own classroom.

1. Which Common Core State Standards for *speaking and listening* do you find trickiest to meet?

2. Which Common Core State Standards for *reading* do you find trickiest to meet?

3. How might pop culture help you meet those standards?

4. What are your concerns?

4 | Using Popular Culture as a Bridge to Complex Texts

In the first chapters, we acknowledged that English language arts (ELA) teachers are not properly trained in when, how, and why to use popular culture as a bridge to access complex literary texts. In this chapter we would like to present scholarly views on the problems or merits of bringing popular culture into classrooms. Upon considering "popular culture camps," we ultimately decide that popular culture provides useful pedagogical tools for our students to learn about literature. We will also present some of our (and others') teaching practices with popular culture. As we do so, we would like to drop pedagogical hints based on our practice. But first, we would like to introduce arguments that oppose bringing popular culture into the classroom. We do so because your attempts to bring popular culture into your curriculum will likely be contested by other teachers, some parents, perhaps your school board, and even some students. You must be prepared to defend your teaching practices. To do so, it helps to know what your detractors might think.

Many Scholars Eschew Popular Culture in the Classroom

Hunt and Hunt (2004) write about their own journey using popular culture in the classroom, specifically discussing Bud Hunt's tension with a hierarchical view of culture—a view that acknowledged that using familiar (popular) texts and cultural information was a strong way to engage students in the classroom:

> [But] he still felt like he was neglecting a piece of his job. That piece was that the English teacher was supposed to connect students with the [elite culture of] books, words, and ideas of faraway places and times. . . . [T]he English

teacher was supposed to wear tweed and recite pithy passages of poetry on demand. The English teacher was to scorn the television, despise all reference to popular culture, and be above that lowly culture enjoyed by the unenlightened masses. The only problem was that Bud was really into that popular culture. (p. 81)

Secondary ELA teachers feel this tension of the debate about what texts should be used to increase students' literacy skills. They hear conflicting messages: One is that using popular culture texts is an effective way to enhance literacy skills, and the other is that restricting the curriculum to simply include texts from the realm of high culture is the only way to teach. The desire to connect the curriculum of the ELA classroom in an engaged and meaningful way, as well as the desire to increase students' literacy skills, is what drives teachers to look for relevant and contextual means to examine popular texts. In addition, both teachers and students are deeply steeped in popular culture, and many enjoy both "elite" and "popular" culture. Yet, such desire and enjoyment does not mean that teachers are inoculated to the debate that occurs between the values of "popular" and "elite" culture, or that such a debate does not influence what curricular decisions are made in the ELA classroom.

Scholarly disparagement of both the mass production and mass consumption of popular culture encountered during teacher education course work may influence how teachers consider incorporating popular texts into their teaching of literature. To illustrate the tension between "elite" and "popular" culture, theorists like Macdonald (1957/2005) argue for elite culture when writing statements like, "Mass Culture is imposed from above. It is fabricated by technicians hired by businessmen; its audiences are passive consumers, their participation limited to the choice between buying and not buying. [The producers of popular culture], in short, exploit the cultural needs of the masses in order to make a profit and/or to maintain their class rule" (Guins & Cruz, 2005, p. 40). Macdonald describes mass culture as both a parasite on high culture and a homogenized product.

Based on this view, mass (or popular) culture, because of the reason and purpose for which it is produced, does not elevate one to a higher experiential level of thinking or feeling like elite culture does, which some say makes the study of popular culture not worthy of students', or teachers', time. As a result of the perceived threat to traditional ideas about culture and art in society based on the role of the technology of mass production and dissemination, the inclusion of particular texts in education—the site many consider to be the front line of cultural transmission—becomes an important part in the debate. Historically, for many scholars who write about popular (or mass) culture, the consensus seems to be that popular culture only serves to pacify and lull people—the masses—into a dull stupor (Adorno & Horkheimer, 1944/2001; Benjamin, 1936/2001; Leavis, 1930/2005;

Macdonald, 1957/2005). As Strinati (1995) explains, "The audience is conceived of [by some scholars] as a mass of passive consumers, prone to the manipulative persuasions of the mass media, submissive to the appeals to buy mass produced commodities made by a mass culture, supine before the false pleasures of mass consumption, and open to the commercial exploitation which motivates mass culture" (p. 12). Similarly, McLuhan (1967) writes, "Print technology created the public. Electric technology created the mass" (p. 68). As seen here, the critique of popular culture comes with a critique of the mass media that creates mass consumption and exploits mass (popular) culture. In his critique of mass media and popular culture, Strinati (1995) writes that some view "the pre-mass society . . . as a communal organic whole in which people accept and abide by a shared and agreed upon set of values which effectively regulate their integration into the community, and which recognise hierarchy and difference" (p. 9). The perceived move from a communal, organic society to an individualized, amoral one is partially the fault of the mass media, some argue, which therefore should have no place in education, especially ELA, historically the site of the transmission of (elite) culture. The argument continues, then, that secondary ELA should (especially) be resistant to the inclusion of popular culture texts and, instead, remain focused on the cultural texts of the literary canon. In this case, the purpose of ELA is to maintain the transmission of elite culture to the uneducated masses of adolescents.

But these scholars do not teach our students. They do not see Matt's students as they are engaged in dissecting and discussing a literary text using the connecting tools of popular culture to forge their textual ideas. This leads us to our first pedagogical insight.

> Pedagogical Insight #1: Articulate your view of popular culture in writing and share it with students. Explain how your thinking is historically situated with prevailing views of popular culture. Then ask students about their views and ask them if access to popular culture has ever helped them gain insight into literary texts. Document their examples.

Teacher Views of Popular Culture Affect Teaching Practices

What ELA teachers think about popular texts affects their teaching practices because we are in the profession of presenting texts to students. A negative or hierarchical view of culture in relation to the role and influence of "elite" culture and "popular" culture shapes how teachers and students interact with traditional academic texts. Those who label Kanye West's "Gold Digger" as "garbage" and F. Scott Fitzgerald's *The Great Gatsby* as "a literary masterpiece" take on this view. Guins and Cruz (2005) write:

> Mass-produced commodities [texts] have been regarded as inauthentic, formulaic, simplistic, and banal. Because they are designed to appeal to global commercial markets rather than reflect the specificity of unique cultural expression, many have and continue to argue that such objects neither challenge aesthetically, morally or spiritually, nor promote active engagement and critical contemplation. (p. 5)

This negative view of mass, or popular, culture as formulaic, simplistic, and banal—as not promoting active or critical thinking—is prevalent among a number of scholars who write about mass and popular culture (Adorno & Horkheimer, 1944/2001; Benjamin, 1936/2001; Leavis, 1930/2005; Macdonald, 1957/2005).

We know from personal experience that popular texts cannot be banned from students' prior knowledge, even in an English class. Kristine grew up on a dairy farm without television or a computer and still learned plenty of information about popular culture through her interactions with peers. If anything, she became *more* interested in television shows, popular movies, popular music, fads, commercials that captured generational zeitgeist, and their advertised products. For most students today, technology makes popular culture even more commonplace. Strinati (1995) writes, "The very fact that culture came to be almost infinitely reproducible due to the development of techniques of industrial production posed considerable problems for traditional ideas about the role of culture and art in society" (p. 4). For many teachers, popular culture might be considered a detriment to society because it is so easily produced and reproducible. That is, everyone has access to popular culture, which, historically, has not been true for elite culture (Berger, 1972; Dewey, 1934).

We think, however, that popular culture is a boon for literary learning precisely because it is so available to American students and offers students common ground for connecting with canonical texts (although students may well take away various opinions regarding the popular text). However, purposeful teachers know *why* they are using the instructional practices they select and can trace their ideas to wider practice. We find the theoretical perspective of Cawelti (2004) helpful in providing teachers with a rationale that popular culture can be a bridge to literature. He observes, "The idea that media *reflect, express,* and *probably reinforce* attitudes and values is a subtler, more flexible, and, in my opinion, more fruitful application of the assumption that the media are involved with values" (p. 64, emphasis added). What Cawelti offers for those who do, and who want to, study mass media and popular culture is a way to ensure that popular culture and mass media are not conflated to mean the same thing, as well as a way to look at popular culture as reflecting, expressing, *and* reinforcing societal values. He shifts the focus from the mass media determining values and behaviors in people to consumers of mass media having agency to make decisions about that media. Cawelti suggests that teachers use a plethora of texts in the classroom and that successful interactions between individual and text, or community and text, depend on the context. His theories echo Langer's (1990) idea that a successful reader makes text-to-world, text-to-text, and text-to-self connections.

Cawelti (2004) makes his view of using a variety of texts in the classroom explicit when he writes:

> One problem with the canon is that the works in it tend to be distanced from us because the living cultural context in which they first appeared is not available to us.
>
> On the other hand, this distancing actually sets a highly creative process into motion insofar as it allows us to discover all kinds of new and complex meanings that remain hidden from us so long as the text only exists in its original cultural space. . . . Our task as teachers is to help foster in young people both a critical understanding of and a sense of discovery and delight in the great works of the past; and I think that popular culture has a key part to play in this process. (p. 128)

So, although many scholars have difficulty in reaching common ground when it comes to defining popular culture and delineating the use and/or presence of popular culture in society, and although a number of teachers feel tension about whether or not to include popular culture in the secondary ELA classroom, an even larger number of teachers and theorists argue for the use of popular culture in education. They recognize that popular culture is being used to some extent already.

At the very beginning of the introduction to his book on theories of popular culture, Strinati (1995) writes, "The study of popular culture is now in the process of becoming a part of the educational curriculum" (p. xiii). That is, many ELA teachers see the use of popular culture in the classroom as a way to increase students' literacy skills and as a way for students to gain access to the literary canon through rich discussions and have already begun to use it. As high-stakes testing and the Common Core State Standards bring more pressure for literacy improvement, and in order to appease outside administrative, governmental, and policy forces, ELA teachers continue to look for new ways that will make certain literacy development, including new ways to help students gain access to traditional literacy skills.

Increasingly, ELA educators are calling for the use of visual, aural, and print texts from the popular culture arena in ELA classrooms as a bridge between the lives of students outside of school and the requirements of academic literacy taught inside of schools. "To be relevant," the New London Group (1996) writes, "learning processes need to recruit, rather than attempt to ignore and erase, the different *subjectivities*—interests, intentions, commitments, and purposes—students bring to learning" (p. 72, emphasis in original). Recruiting subjectivities, in this case, means tapping into the literacy—and literary—practices with which students already engage. Indeed, many teachers are recognizing the need to make connections between the literacy practices students participate in outside of school and the literacy practices mandated inside of school. Hobbs and Frost (2003) write:

> Scholars who situate literacy within the contexts of culture and child development argue that the range and diversity of 'texts' used in the classroom must be expanded to include artifacts of popular culture. These scholars identify a range of potential outcomes, such as the following: (a) to increase learning by making the practices of literacy relevant to students' home cultures and ways of knowing . . . (b) to accommodate diverse learning styles and meet the needs of multicultural learners . . . and (c) to develop creativity, self-expression, teamwork, and workplace skills. (p. 330)

The International Reading Association (IRA) and the National Council of Teachers of English (NCTE) have also joined in the call for the use of popular culture texts: "Being literate in contemporary society means being active, critical, and creative users of print and spoken language, as well as the visual language of film and television, commercial and political advertising, and more" (quoted in Asselin, 2001, p. 47; and Morrell, 2002, p. 75). It would seem, then, that using popular culture texts in the classroom is a viable option for teachers as they work to improve students' literacy skills and as they work to respond to the debate over what such improvement is or should be.

Pedagogical Insight #2: As you construct learning targets for literary lessons from the Common Core, consider how popular texts might offer students access into complex texts. Before you analyze a canonical text, consider scaffolding analytical thinking to a popular text first. We offer examples later in this chapter.

Alright, Enough Theory: How Do I Do This?

While the previous pages have probably felt like a lot of theory, we believe master teachers need theory to explain their actions. We felt that it was important to acknowledge and explore the historical debates and discussions that have taken place around the idea of, and topic of, culture and popular culture. As Kathryn has discovered in her classes, pre-service and in-service teachers are ready and willing to acknowledge their interaction with popular texts and technologies, but they have difficulty talking about it because they lack vocabulary or themes for discussion. They are quick to talk about which television shows are better than others (critical and complex thinking), but they sometimes have difficulty giving words or language to that debate. For example, they like to compare *New Girl* with *The Mindy Project*, debating the characters, the humor, and the plots. They like to argue the merits of both shows. But, the important fact is that *students are already thinking critically about popular culture*. Students are *already* demonstrating complex literacy (reading, writing, thinking, speaking) skills in the ways they talk about popular culture. As Morrell (2004) writes, "[Students] already possess many of the skills that we, as educators, want to impart to them. However, by not allowing them to tap into their huge reservoirs of knowledge, we also prevent many from incorporating these skills into their engagements with traditional texts" (p. 87). The question, then, is how to help students replicate their skills with (popular) language and literacy with the language and literacy of (canonical) complex texts of the ELA classroom.

We mentioned earlier that the tensions with incorporating popular culture texts have to do with the assumption that such an incorporation demeans the literary canon, such an incorporation is difficult because of the fast-paced changes within popular culture, and such an incorporation feels like an intrusion into students' popular culture (their "private" or "safe" space). Often, even though students are already thinking and speaking about popular culture in complex ways, they don't know that they are doing so.

> Pedagogical Insight #3: Inventory your students' consumption of popular culture. This is valuable information in planning curriculum. Ask particularly articulate students to do "think-alouds" in front of their peers as they analyze popular texts. Document their practices. The same practices may work well when students analyze literature.

Morrell (2004) suggests finding reliable student informants who are willing to share current trends, texts, and practices. In addition, a method Kathryn uses at the beginning of every semester of new students is to distribute a literacy survey (Figure 4.1) that students fill out the first day of class (sometimes due the second day of class).

Included with this survey are other "getting to know you" questions, such as:

- What are you most excited about this year/semester?
- What do you think will be the most challenging thing for you this year/semester?
- Are you involved in any extracurricular activities?
- What do I need to know about you as a learner (reader, writer, speaker, listener)?

In asking such questions, and by discussing students' responses as a class, not only is there time to get to know one another and have an organized way to do so,

Instructions

Listed below are 20 literacy-related activities. If you engage in a particular activity at home, indicate by placing a check in the blank under the "home" heading. "Home" means any place other than school. If you engage in a particular activity at school, indicate by placing a check in the blank under the "school" heading. If you engage in a particular activity both in and out of school, place a check in the blank under both headings.

Activity	Home	School	Rank
1. Read a book	_____	_____	_____
2. Write a story	_____	_____	_____
3. Read a newspaper	_____	_____	_____
4. Watch a movie	_____	_____	_____
5. Listen to music	_____	_____	_____
6. Look at works of art	_____	_____	_____
7. Read a magazine	_____	_____	_____
8. Write poetry	_____	_____	_____
9. Read poetry	_____	_____	_____
10. Chat on the Internet	_____	_____	_____
(instant messaging, text messaging, includes cell phones)			
11. Write notes to friends	_____	_____	_____
(includes text messaging on cell phones)			
12. Research on the Internet	_____	_____	_____
13. Attend concerts	_____	_____	_____
14. Draw or paint	_____	_____	_____
15. Watch television	_____	_____	_____
16. Read instruction booklets/manuals	_____	_____	_____
17. Write music	_____	_____	_____
18. Attend plays or musicals	_____	_____	_____
19. Use the computer for email	_____	_____	_____
20. Read comics/graphic novels	_____	_____	_____
21. Write in a journal	_____	_____	_____
22. Write a speech	_____	_____	_____
23. Write a newspaper article/ editorial	_____	_____	_____
24. Write a research report	_____	_____	_____
25. Conduct an interview	_____	_____	_____

Figure 4.1 Literacy survey.

(Continued)

Once you have completed that, place a ☺ *next to your five most favorite activities and a* ☹ *next to your five least favorite activities.*

Next, answer the following questions:

1. What do you most enjoy about your five most favorite activities?

2. What do you least enjoy about your five least favorite activities?

3. Think about your most favorite English assignment. What did you most enjoy about that assignment?

4. Think about your least favorite English assignment. What did you least enjoy about that assignment?

5. What is your first memory that includes a book? What is your first memory that includes a movie? What is your first memory that includes a TV show?

6. List your current favorites and note why your selection appeals to you:
   MOVIE:
   TV SHOW:
   BOOK (COMIC/GRAPHIC NOVEL):
   SONG AND MUSICAL ARTIST:
   WEBSITE:
   VIDEO/ONLINE GAME:
   FASHION/CLOTHING ITEM:

but there is also the chance to establish some common language around literacy and text in addition to having some common examples to which to refer. As a result, we, as teachers and students, take that "first important step in [the] transformative process [of] learning to see all students as learners and users of language and literacy before they even enter the classroom" (Morrell, 2004, p. 6). For example, Kathryn's current semester began with quite a bit of discussion about Miley Cyrus' performance at the 2013 MTV Video Music Awards. In experiencing this cultural event, either through direct viewing or through conversations the next day, Kathryn and her students had the chance to discuss the negative reception of Cyrus' performance, look at examples of rhetoric surrounding it, and practice having thoughtful conversations about power, gender, culture, and popular culture. One of the most important parts of all of this was that Kathryn got a glimpse into what her students knew *and* got a glimpse of what cultural texts her students liked. She therefore, with her class, had a place to start conversations about art, culture, and texts and the issues that are part of them.

> Pedagogical Insight #4: Make a video of an early conversation about a popular text. Reflect on Common Core State Standard verbs that students use to make sense of popular texts. Are they "describing" the text or are they "critiquing" the text? What kinds of probes might you ask to get students to the kind of thinking you are looking for? What common language do you want students to take out of these discussions that can be applied to literary discussions?

Consider the following Common Core standards for literary reading and the verbs that are used (the verbs are in boldface).

- RL.7.1. **Cite** several pieces of textual evidence to support analysis of what the text says explicitly as well as inferences drawn from the text.

- RL.7.2. **Determine** a theme or central idea of a text and analyze its development over the course of the text; **provide** an objective summary of the text.

- RL.7.3. **Analyze** how particular elements of a story or drama interact (e.g., how setting shapes the characters or plot).

- RL.7.4. **Determine** the meaning of words and phrases as they are used in a text, including figurative and connotative meanings; **analyze** the impact of rhymes and other repetitions of sounds (e.g., alliteration) on a specific verse or stanza of a poem or section of a story or drama.

- RL.7.5. **Analyze** how a drama's or poem's form or structure (e.g., soliloquy, sonnet) contributes to its meaning.

- RL.7.6. **Analyze** how an author develops and contrasts the points of view of different characters or narrators in a text.

If your learning target for a discussion about a popular text is RL.7.1, "cite" is the action you want students to demonstrate during the discussion. You want students to quote from several passages you are reading in a manner that shows they understood the passage. Their quotes should be lifted directly from the text you are discussing or should show their inferencing skills of reading between the lines of the text. If students are not citing the text, it would be wise to prompt them to lift words, phrases, sentences, and paragraphs from the text and explain what they mean in their own words or offer a scenario from real life where they must apply the meaning of the text to a real-world situation.

Thinking About Standards in a Broader Sense

Of course our learning targets do not just come from the standards mentioned above for literary reading. Part of every ELA classroom is a focus on language—whether the language of writing, of speaking, of reading, or of listening. Common Core standard CCRA.R.4 states that students should "interpret words and phrases as they are used in a text, including determining technical, connotative, and figurative meanings, and analyze how specific word choices shape meaning or tone." One activity that Kathryn does with her students during the first week of school is a critical analysis of an advertisement. Given that we see, depending on the latest statistic, close to 5,000 advertisements a day, learning to interpret words and images, learning connotative and figurative meanings, and analyzing how word and image choices shape meaning are important moves to make. But it is the way in which a close reading of an advertisement opens up discussion of how to do a close reading of a (canonical) text that is important in Kathryn's classroom. In groups of three or four students, each group chooses one advertisement (Kathryn usually gives each group two or three ads to choose from) and answers the following questions (Kathryn uses key terms from Bloom's Taxonomy, in boldface):

- Specifically **name** the message of the advertisement. **Describe** what the ad is literally trying to sell.
- **Outline** the language used to do this.
- **Describe** how the visual image is used to do this.
- **Analyze** the hidden meaning. What is the literal story being told? What is the hidden story being told? **Point out** evidence for your answer.
- **Judge** the effectiveness of the ad. Does the ad work for you? Why or why not?

Through this activity, Kathryn and her students not only begin the year practicing a critical reading of a text, but they also establish common questions and common language that they can then apply to other texts as the school year continues. Thus, as Kathryn introduces texts that are longer and more complex, students remember and can refer to the verbs and questions they applied to the shorter texts of advertisements.

The question remains, though, of how to help students gain and develop the skills of close reading. Part of this question, too, is how to help students see an incorporation of popular culture not just as a "fun" activity, but also as a way to practice Common Core standard CCRA.R.1: "Read closely to determine what the text says explicitly and to make logical inferences from it; cite specific textual evidence when writing or speaking to support conclusions drawn from the text." Again, a good place to start is to have students practice what they already know. For example, by showing the opening sequence of the films *The Godfather* and *The Matrix*, students can talk about characterization, setting, tone, and interpretation. That is, by watching the opening sequences and then discussing all they know and interpret just by watching the first few minutes of the movie, they are practicing a close, inferential reading. What follows are some popular text and literature connections that we think are useful:

- *Secret Window* (2004)——Edgar Allan Poe
- *The Simpson's* "The Raven"——Edgar Allan Poe
- *Of Mice and Men* (1992)——text
- *The Mighty* (1998)——*Of Mice and Men*
- *The Crucible* (1996)——text
- *Fried Green Tomatoes* (1991)——text
- *10 Things I Hate About You* (1999)——*Taming of the Shrew*
- *The Princess Bride* (1987) as an example of the archetypal hero
- Clips from *Saving Private Ryan* (1998)——*All Quiet on the Western Front*
- *In Love and War* (1996)——*All Quiet on the Western Front*
- *Star Wars* (1977)——*Beowulf*
- Billy Joel's "We Didn't Start the Fire" (1989)——*Brave New World*
- John Lennon's "Imagine" (1975)——*Brave New World*
- *Pleasantville* (1998)——*The Giver*
- *The Truman Show* (1998)——*The Giver*

Matt Uses Popular Texts as a Bridge to a Canonical Text

What follows is Matt's application of our four pedagogical tips in the chapter. In the vignettes below, the popular texts that scaffold literary thinking are musical lyrics. When students began to share about their prior knowledge with music, they made connections to what it means to be an individual in a society that values conformity even when it means being "different like everybody else." Camazotz, a setting in *A Wrinkle in Time*, offered students insight into a world where everyone thought and moved in synchronized movement without thought. It was, or became, a place where evil flourished unbeknownst to law-abiding citizens because they had not learned to question tyrannical authority. The themes of the literary text reflect, express, and reinforce societal values in lyrics that students are already familiar with, especially the students placed in the music and conformity discussion group based on their interest in music.

The music group, composed of Neo, Jacqueline, and James, wanted to examine what it means to be an individual. After consulting with Matt, these students are leading a whole-class discussion in front of their peers. Neo, who highly values non-conformity as a character trait, initiates the first question for his peers:

Neo: I want to ask you a question now. How do people show individuality? What do you see in people that makes them unique from other people? Caroline?

Caroline: [Ironically] Well, whichever one swears the most obviously makes them the most individual.

Indigo: People might dye their hair or wear crazy clothes—that way they won't look like everyone else.

Jacqueline: Do you think that music reflects individuality? And how does it help you in your life sort of?

Harry: Well, I think there's a lot of different music. Like there's classic, hip hop, whatever. So basically, if you want to listen to that, maybe it can go with your mood or whatever. So, everyone has a different kind of music.

Caroline: Sometimes you can relate to experiences described in the song. A popular topic in songs nowadays is breakup. So oftentimes you can listen to those and maybe relate to it.

James: Like "Boyfriend" by Justin Bieber.

Caroline observes that words, even swear words, can make people stand out from the crowd. So can a change in appearance, as Indigo observes. And so can music. Music can be selected to coordinate with one's mood or what is happening, or has happened, in one's life. Students demonstrate Reader Response attitudes (see Chapter 1) toward the music in their lives. Listeners matter when listening to music. They are powerful agents in the transactions among musical performer, lyrics and melody, and listener. In fact, music can be an identity marker. All of this talk is allowing important student prior knowledge to come to the surface.

Later in the discussion, a student, Nolan, participates in a think-aloud and initiates his insight that expression of individuality through music should involve competence and artistry and not be quickly produced to offer empty messages to undiscriminating consumers.

Nolan: I kind of have something. Like how music has changed in a way, I don't know if this is a little off topic. But, uh, I notice that, like, a while ago you had to work a lot harder for stuff, so it was more safe songs because they weren't really into funny or popularity yet, and it slowly got to the point where some people don't really work at all, and they get a lot of money still. So it's like songs are current.

James: What are some examples? Do you know any?

Nolan: Well, you know, if you go a hundred years back, you can only hear classical songs. But if you go up here, there's eight different or thirty different songs.

Nolan is offering a powerful criticism about his time. Musical popularity may be about being new rather than about being good. Success may not require effort and talent. This does not sit well with Nolan, who seems to indicate that artistry should require effort and skill. Note how James has asked Nolan for "some examples." This cue is urging him to cite an important verb at work in this discussion.

Later in the discussion, music is ultimately tied to Camazotz, a place of peace at first glance but actually of conformity. The class discusses whether peace with conformity is worth the absence of individual identity. A student engaged in metaphorical thinking contrasts popcorn with a lollipop and observes that the popcorn makes the lollipop sweeter, attempting to make the point that a variety of taste sensations is necessary in order to recognize the sweetness of life. Other students observe that some individual nonconformists harm society, but Nolan notes that perfection would create boredom. After hashing out conformity versus individuality, the class agrees that their world has gone too far in trying to conform *and* too far in trying to make individuals stand out at times when a team effort is needed to keep society safe and running smoothly for the benefit of most. The discourse is fitting for adolescents who will hopefully spend their adult lives in a system of democracy that requires constant attention to balancing the need of the individual versus the rights of the group.

The focus on individuality through music provides space for students to analyze and critique their collective culture. It should be noted that the day the music group facilitates their discussion, Matt is absent, although he has approved of the questions the group will present to the class, questions that allow views on popular culture to be revealed. Students are feeling their oats a bit with the substitute teacher, and yet learning happens almost in spite of themselves.

Neo: Our activity is to see how many pop culture singers you can name in one minute.
Student: Yay!
Caroline: Do they have to be singers or can they be bands?
James: They can be bands.
Chelle: Can they be not from this culture? Like Japanese?
Neo: We're going to start in a few seconds. Are you guys ready? [He looks at Tiana, whose role is to write down the list that the class constructs.]
James: We have two minutes on the clock.

Several singers and bands are noted:

One Direction

Beatles

Adele

Queen

Justin Bieber

Selena Gomez

Taylor Swift

The Presidents of the United States of America

Hannah Montana

Pink Floyd

Oprah

Lady Gaga

The Monkees

The Beach Boys

Although Neo's hook to the discussion is loud and noisy, students demonstrate total engagement in the activity. The stage is set to go deeper. Now James takes the lead.

James:	Look at all of these groups up here. Why do you think people like this music?
Chelle:	It's very pleasing to the ears and it's fun to listen to.
Caroline:	Because . . . the Beatles. I think their songs have good lyrics.
Neo:	So why do you think the Beatles were successful? What do you think made them successful?
Caroline:	Because they were considered hot in their time.
Neo:	Chase?
Chase:	I feel they got famous because people at school that are cool [his fingers form quotation marks around the word "cool"] listen to them.
Neo:	Anything else? Like, why do you think people today like pop culture? What do you think makes pop culture? What's the definition of pop culture?
Caroline:	Pop culture is something that celebrities made up for a way for them to be able to keep making money. And if everybody ignored the secret to losing fifty pounds in two weeks or how Rihanna lost thirty pounds on a special diet, if everyone just stopped paying attention to that kind of thing, then pop culture would just flat drop.
Chase:	It creates interesting conversation between one or more people, and it just creates differences, and people want differences because that's what's happening in the celebrity world.
Chelle:	Because it kind of gives people something to look up to. Like if you take away all the celebrities and stuff, then we'd have no one to idolize. So we'd all just sit there and be confused.

Neo:	Those are all excellent points. Now taking it back to old school. Take, for example, Beethoven and Bach, what do you think made them special? They were considered pop culture back then. What made them individual and unique?
Chelle:	They had talent.
Caroline:	Because . . . I'm using Beethoven as an example. He went deaf towards the end of his career, and they probably thought that was pretty amazing back then that he was able to do that.
Neo:	So now in pop culture people just like people because of their money and their fame and their looks. But back then, it was inspirational for people to follow Bach, I mean Beethoven, because he went deaf but he still kept on pushing himself.
Harry:	Probably because they actually had talent. But now you just go into the studio, even if your voice was really bad, they can make it into something good. [A student shouts out "autotune!"]
James:	Think of the top ten songs of now and the 1980s and their differences. In the 1980s, all the songs were about nice things and today half the songs have explicit lyrics. Why the change?
Caroline:	As the standards of society change, so do the standards for music.
Nolan:	[Looking at the top ten songs of today] These songs are all about popularity.

These students are engaging their peers in meaningful dialogue and demonstrate presentation skills valued in the workplace. Neo knows to start with a hook, an important presentation skill. Tiana knows to document responses. Students argue about why musicians become famous (because they have talent, because they are popular with the right group, because they are inspirational, because they are hot). The discussants observe that cultural artifacts of a time period reflect the concerns of the society from which the artifact emerged. In their culture, Nolan notes, popularity is an important theme. Students harken back to the good old days of Beethoven, who inspired society in his day, and the hits of the 1980s, when lyrics were "nice" (Tipper Gore disagreed). So much critical thinking is happening, and all of this happens on a less than optimal day when a substitute teacher is present.

The setting of Camazotz and themes of conformity become throughlines in Matt's class. Initially, when students first read about the peaceful place earlier in the unit, some found Camazotz compelling. After an initial reading of a description of Camasotz, a student observes that it seems like a perfect place. Leo immediately disagrees, showing his ability to interpret the world and make predictions of literary text. His interpretations are based on his prior knowledge of popular culture, i.e., *Battlestar Galactica*.

Leo:	Unless they overdo it and everything has to be exactly the same. And in a book, I think, this is the first time I've seen where everything is all the same.

Brendon: Actually there's a sentence where a big wall opens up and all the scientists are working together with the machines. And everyone inside the Central Intelligence Agency are just the same. They're like programmed in a way.

Leo: A movie that I saw it in was *Battlestar Galactica*. Everyone was the same. All the thingies . . . cylons.

Matt: [To the whole class, changing the tenor of discussion] How would you feel if you were forced to live there?

Leo: I'd be so scared.

Brendon: I would freak out. [There is a lot of agreement by his peers.]

Leo: I think the word used to describe this place is aberrations. If you're sub-normal, you're weird. Or if you're not the same as everyone else, you're hated. And you'll be taken away.

Brendon: I think I'd hide in a corner or freak out.

Matt has the class think of story lines in popular culture in which conformity caused harmony or conflict. Students mention Willy Wonka and the Oompa Loompas, who look and act alike, causing his factory to run. They recall the little green toy soldiers from *Toy Story*, whose synchronized action is noble. Another student remembers an episode in the cartoon *Arthur* in which character(s) copied and pasted assignments and got a good grade. Others specify *Finding Nemo* and the little fishes forming shapes to protect the group, and Pac-Man, where conformity causes loss of individual identity. And then James shows a video of Pink Floyd's *Another Brick in the Wall*. As most of the class had never seen the video, they are riveted and wanted to talk about what it means.

James: I have a video. It's by Pink Floyd and it's called *Another Brick in the Wall*. And in the UK, the schooling back then, it was really harsh. And teachers were really strict, and you couldn't talk and [had to take] rigorous notes and stuff and it was really hard. At the age of twelve they decided what your career path would be. That's really hard because you don't mature at age twelve. You mature at age twenty. And so that can change the rest of your life. This video is pretty weird. It shows kids lining up and going into a blender and then coming out.

Caroline: It's Pink Floyd!

James: And it's just a song about how schooling is really bad and how they don't like it.

James is right about the video (although perhaps not about the maturing age). The video shows the harshness of school as a factory that turns young adolescents into soulless sausages. After the movie, students rush to make sense of the popular text by describing what they saw and explicating its meaning and the video choices used to make the point about a dehumanizing educational system.

James: It's because children in the UK, they had no individuality because school
            was so harsh.
Chase: Why did they come out in orange strips?
Caroline: I was thinking about them being molded into society.
Chase: That's a gruesome way to put that. I don't think they needed to go to that
            extent of, like, shredding kids.
Chelle: Basically it's like overemphasizing a point. If they don't address the point,
            then people won't listen. So, by going to drastic measures to prove their
            point, it worked.
Chase: It made it stick in people's mind, I'll tell you that much. It's not lecturing,
            but they went a little over the top.
James: Schooling was terrible back then. It was like Camazotz.

Camazotz has become part of the students' collective schema, a reference point of a place that strips people of humanity and individuality. Literature allows the students in class to assimilate a mostly unfamiliar artifact from popular culture into their existing frameworks of individuality and conformity.

On another day, Matt shows a clip of *The Truman Show* to the class. He wants the students to do literary analysis by comparing two settings using textual evidence. He asks the class, "What makes that world created for Truman similar to Camazotz? How are they similar? What I would ask you to do is to give me examples from the story and examples from the movie that prove your point." They are eager to do so.

Celia: Well, they're both artificial. They can't live their own lives.
Matt: Good.
Haven: In Camazotz they do everything the exact same way day in and day out 365
            days of the year and most likely it's the same for Truman. He does the same
            exact routine every day. He says good morning and goodbye.
Matt: So we have sameness, we have artificiality. How are they different?
Leo: They're different because in Camazotz they all know what's happening—
            like when the boy drops the ball, the mom actually gets scared and in the
            movie he has no clue what's happening, so, like when the light drops, he
            didn't know what was happening.
Matt: So [Celia], you said they are both artificial. Can you give me evidence from
            the book and from the movie that proves it is artificial?
Celia: Well, for Truman, the whole thing is made up. It's a set. And for Camazotz,
            everyone does the exact same thing. So if you can't be yourself, then it's
            pretty artificial, I think.
Matt: So you both did literary analysis. So writing it down is the same.

Comparison and contrast thinking can be difficult, especially for young adolescents who tend to be concrete thinkers because of their developmental level. Yet text-to-text connections can be mediated when one text is a film and engages more senses than traditional texts. The discourse of the students above can easily be morphed into the substance of a comparison and contrast essay, a valued genre in secondary school. The student writing introduced in Chapter 7 is evidence of the scaffolding role of literature discussion in showing Matt's students that they have wisdom to share with the troubled celebrities who dominate much of popular culture.

What the discourse of the student demonstrates in the vignettes above is that students are engaging in several Common Core targets for reading literature. They do cite textual evidence to support what the text says implicitly and explicitly. They can determine the theme of a text over time and provide an objective summary of it. They can analyze how elements of a story interact. The textual discussion of students indicates that Matt's class is a robust learning environment.

Opportunity for Reflection

Consider how you might apply the ideas from this chapter to your own classroom.

1. What is your view of popular culture in the ELA classroom? Based on your experiences as a student and teacher, why do you hold this view?

2. Has popular culture helped your students develop literary insight? Why or why not? Has popular culture impeded literary insight? Why or why not?

3. How might you use analytical thinking to examine a popular text? What processes of thinking could be transferred to analyzing literature?

4. When students perform think-alouds as they make meaning from popular texts, what reading strategies do they use? Can you use students' authentic strategies as a classroom resource? How?

5. Select a learning target for a class in which discussion is one activity for learning. Do the verbs of the learning target map onto the conversational turns of students? Why or why not?

5 | What Rich Discussion Looks Like and How to Set It Up

In this chapter we would like to demonstrate what good textual discussion looks like, offer ideas and insights for how to set it up in the classroom, and suggest thoughts for assessment. We take you inside Matt's classrooms while he teaches a unit in which students read and discuss with sophisticated insight Madeleine L'Engle's *A Wrinkle in Time*. We illustrate that Matt's instructional decision making that allows time and space for permeable textual discussions, in which students connect popular culture to their own lives, can be defended with Common Core speaking and listening standards. Although students have pseudonyms, their comments while engaged in literature discussions are their actual words. By the end of this chapter, we hope we have demonstrated the sophisticated cognitive skills of middle school students who think deeply about literature. As we describe Matt's unit, we want to unpack what Matt is doing in a particular unit so you can borrow from his thinking as you plan your own literature discussions. Note our pedagogical insights throughout the chapter.

A Bit More Background on Matt and a Situated Literature Unit

Even though Matt teaches in Seattle, Washington, he considers Texas, where he grew up, the place where much of his identity was formed. His classroom is decorated with jerseys of his favorite Texas team, the Mavericks. Whenever he can, Matt weaves in aspects of growing up in Texas, where he attended an all-boys school. Throughout the unit, he makes text-to-self connections with the main characters in *A Wrinkle in Time*. His class enjoys his stories of when he had to visit the principal two times for forging a love note and for pulling a prank on a neighboring school for girls. Because stories lead to more stories, and he is open and interested in the stories of his students, he creates a classroom atmosphere where he is known and where students are comfortable to know each other. His classroom becomes optimal for new learning because revealing personal literary insight may feel like a risk to an adolescent and the discomfort of new learning must be balanced with the comfort of being known.

> Pedagogical Insight #1: Stories beget stories. If you really want students to apply literature to their own lives in meaningful ways, a teacher has to value student stories and regard them as important resources for learning. But when telling your own stories, you should connect them to literature and make those connections explicit. This is compatible with Speaking and Listening Target SL.7.2: Explain how ideas clarify a topic or text.

It is spring and Matt is scheduled to teach *A Wrinkle in Time* to his seventh graders. The fantasy/science fiction Newbery-award winning text has been much censored in schools and libraries because of overt religious themes that have been much contested by fundamentalist Christians and atheists and others in between the two religious spectrums. Author Madeleine L'Engle was a devout Christian, and it shows in her religious textual references. L'Engle was also open about honoring non-Christian worldviews in which love, creativity, kindness, and excellence are emphasized.

> Pedagogical Insight #2: Controversial texts can work well with stimulating discussion about the worth of a text where students need to make and defend claims about textual themes. This is compatible with Speaking and Listening Target SL.7.3: Unpack arguments and claims, evaluating the soundness of reasoning and evidence.

In the novel, gawky Meg Murray is having personal and community identity conflicts. Her father, a renowned scientist, has disappeared; her frail brother, Charles Wallace, is being picked on at school; and Meg is in trouble at school for arguing with teachers who show their ignorance of science and think she is unintelligent because she is not a traditional learner. During "a dark and stormy night," a strange personage by the name of Mrs. Who appears at her door and eventually leads Meg, her younger brother Charles, and their friend Calvin O'Keefe on an adventure between worlds. With the help of otherworldly friends, the children discover that Mr. Murray has been captured by the Dark Thing. The children must travel to an alternate universe, Camazotz, and confront the leader of conformity, IT, in an epic battle of good and evil. Meg realizes in risking her life to save her family that love is the most powerful force in the universe. The longevity of the novel has much to do with compelling themes that resonate with adolescents: finding one's family and personal identity, conformity, young love, and bullying.

Although 50 years old in 2012, the children's literature classic is still taught in many upper elementary and middle school classrooms. But this year, Matt wants students to make more personal connections with the book. The students are each given a book they are to annotate to further their reading comprehension. They are to engage in active reading and jot down interesting things that come to their minds as they read: what they find interesting or confusing, connections they make with passages and real life, words they do not understand, questions they have with passages in the book.

Pedagogical Insight #3: Students will be more likely to create rich literature discussion at the first discussion phase if they can provide textual support for making exploratory claims, which means that reading and writing should preface literature discussions. They need to do their "research" first (SL.7.1) and refer to their research to support their exploratory literary claims (SL.7.1).

To set a purpose for the first few chapters of the book and to show they have created envisionment with the characters in the introductory chapters, Matt asks students to try to identify characters from the movies and television that they would cast in their roles and why they connect those actors with the characters. The following day, students are ready to talk. Some students note that the principal from *Ant Farm*, a popular pre-teen show, would make a good Mr. Jenkins, the principal in *A Wrinkle in Time*. But beyond making connections to Mr. Jenkins' appearance, they have some difficulty supporting their choice based on passages from the text. A few people dominate this whole-class discussion. Most students who comment on Meg's character portray her in a negative light. It is clear that students are reading the words of the novel but not thinking as deeply as they might. There is cognitive work to be done for literary analysis worthy of preparing students to be college and career ready.

Pedagogical Insight #4: Teachers should establish "pre-test" measures for a baseline assessment of the quality of class discussions. Video or audiotape can capture these data. At the end of a unit of study, this pre-test data can be compared with "post-test" measures to inform teachers whether student speaking and listening skills have improved. We highly recommend that excerpts of video or audio be shared with students along with teacher rubrics noting particular discussion events as teaching examples so that students can be intentional in working on their speaking and listening skills.

From the first day of the unit, upon perusal of student talk, it is clear that certain speaking and listening standards should be focus learning targets for this unit. Among them, a few jump out at us as particularly necessary in scaffolding speaking and listening that is college and career ready:

(1) Students should be able to demonstrate discourse in which they build on the ideas of others (SL.7.1).

(2) Students should be able to probe others so they can reflect upon text (SL.7.1).

(3) Students should be able to follow the rules of liberal discourse where everyone can contribute and defend their opinions (SL.7.1).

(4) Students should be able to modify their opinions about text when others share information that might help to change their minds (SL.7.1).

(5) Students should be able to unpack arguments and claims, evaluating the soundness of reasoning and evidence (SL.7.3).

Once speaking and speaking and listening targets have been organically determined by student talk, teachers can form simple rubrics they can return to throughout

Unit Title:
Discussion Topic:
Length of Discussion:
Circle One: Pretest   Mid-unit   Post-test

Speaking and listening learning target	Specific evidence from student talk that target is being met or unmet (video or audio time)	Reflection on student talk for future improvement or commendation
Students should be able to demonstrate discourse in which they build on the ideas of others.		
Students should be able to probe others so they can reflect upon text.		
Students should be able to follow the rules of liberal discourse where everyone can contribute and defend their opinions.		
Students should be able to modify their opinions about text when others share information that might help to change their mind.		
Students should be able to unpack arguments and claims, evaluating the soundness of reasoning and evidence.		

Figure 5.1 Sample discussion rubric.

the unit to establish whether progress is being made. The rubric in Figure 5.1 can be used as a template.

Matt places all of the students in discussion groups so they can practice their discussion facilitation skills in small groups. Each group is to lead a Thursday discussion that will last 20 minutes to half an hour and will consist of targeted, student-led discussion accompanied by media clips and student-generated activities to inspire rich discussion. Matt has assigned students to groups based on his knowledge of their identities and interests: a "girl power" and movies group, a music and individuality group, and a superheroes and celebrities group. Vignettes from the girl power and movies group will provide illustrations for the rest of this chapter.

 Pedagogical Insight #5: Units in which small-group and large-group formats are used allow more speaking and listening targets to be met.

Matt's lesson planning provides opportunities for multiple Common Core speaking and listening standards to be addressed: instructional variety (7.1), student research that contributes to discussion (7.1), student-generated textual questions (7.1), clear discussion topics (7.1), presentation of student claims and findings (7.4), desirable public speaking verbal and nonverbal communication such as eye contact, volume, and pronunciation (7.4), use of multimedia components to clarify claims and add emphasis to student talk (7.5), and opportunities for students to use formal English (7.6).

Girl Power Groups Demonstrate Rich Discussion

In the following vignette, Matt has just introduced the members of the "Girl Power." They have not yet begun to read *A Wrinkle in Time*. The group has already spent some time talking about the best example of girl power they have encountered in popular culture, particularly Katniss from *The Hunger Games*. The movie has just arrived in theatres and many students have seen it and/or read the book.

Matt poses a few introductory questions to the group. They are asked to use their connections to "go deep" so that their exploratory talk of popular culture can create a framework for what girl power means. Discussion questions are written down to keep the discussion on track. First, Matt asks the small group to think of a real-life example of girl power. Several seconds of silence ensue. Lindy thinks of Amelia Earhart, but her group members are not too excited about the example. They move on to the next question.

Blake: What does the term "girl power" mean to you, Roxy?
Roxy: Girls can do whatever guys can do.

Blake:	Let's go deeper [smirking a bit].
Roxy:	*You* go deeper. You haven't answered yet.
Blake:	Yah I did. Okay I will. Girl power means that girls can do whatever they put their mind to if they work hard. And guys who are usually lazy and slacking off get it pretty easy just cuz they're guys. And girls, because they're working, are better.
Roxy:	Cassandra?
Cassandra:	The same thing. If they put their mind to it.
Lindy:	Yah. If they work really hard, then they can do anything guys can do. And maybe most likely be better at it.

Pedagogical Insight #6: Opportunities for exploratory writing compatible with upcoming and planned discussion topics (i.e., asking the group members to produce a list of strong women and girls and their personal characteristics via a t-chart) would likely lead to richer small-group talk. Accessing important prior knowledge and orally communicating it to others is not always immediate for some students.

Although students know their discussion has to "go deep" and come up with a working definition of girl power, a goal that needs to be accomplished as part of the group, they have not had adequate time to go deep by presenting claims about girl power in a coherent manner (SL.7.4) and unpacking why particular girls and women demonstrate characteristics of girl power (7.3). Preliminary research is in order. At the same time, prior knowledge of Katniss helps them formulate a simple response that can be built on later. Students can track their discussion insights through writing.

Pedagogical Insight #7: Discussions should be compatible with unit writing tasks, as both instructional practices usually mutually reinforce each other. Students will have more to discuss, as we have noted above, if they have clarified their thinking through writing. Students will have more to write about a topic, especially knowledge of disagreement about individually held literary claims, if a topic has been discussed thoroughly by group members.

After reading the first few chapters of *A Wrinkle in Time*, the girl power group met again to create connections with characters using popular culture references. They respond to two questions Matt has initiated:

(1) (Character in the first few chapters) reminds me of . . . and

(2) When (plot action occurred in the first few chapters), I was reminded of . . .

This time students first write their responses on paper and exchange them. Because they have written their responses to a prompt, this time everyone has something to say. The advanced warning of discussion topics and time for reflective writing aids the small-group discussions to be more meaningful. The ensuing discussion helps Cassandra realize that she was confusing two characters, Charles Wallace and Calvin O'Keefe.

Cassandra: Charles reminds me of sports athletes.
Blake: Charles?
Cassandra: Isn't he sporty?
Roxy: Not Charles. Calvin.
Cassandra: Okay, Calvin reminds me of athletes. They're like big and stuff. And then, the second question, how Charles read Meg's mind, reminds me of Edward [from *Twilight*].
Blake: He does?
Lindy: I put Meg just reminds me of the Ugly Duckling because everyone thinks she's ugly at the beginning but she might turn out good at the end. And then I put Sandy and Dennis remind me of the twins in *Alice in Wonderland* because they're just alike and stuff . . .
Roxy: I feel bad for Meg because she's going to have bad teenage years.
Lindy: Yeah. Then Charles reminds me of some magic person.
Blake: The genie from *Aladdin*!
Lindy: He could just tell what you want and how you are doing and stuff.

The young women show their connections with characters from a wide repertoire of resources: recent books and movies, classic children's stories, canonical texts, Disney movies. This important knowledge creates envisionment with major characters. Connections quickly become more personal for Roxy, who sees herself as a person with a complex personality.

Roxy: I'm like Meg, Charles Wallace, and Mrs. Whatsit. I'm kind of like Charles because I like to know words that people don't. I'm like Meg because I'm a little clumsy. I'm like Mrs. Whatsit because sometimes people think I'm a little crazy.

Another girl power group in another class who make completely different connections with popular culture are able to defend their choices, amending them and clarifying their visualizations as they speak (SL.7.1).

Caroline: So I thought Meg was kind of like Frodo Baggins from [*The*] *Lord of the Rings* because Bilbo's parental figure goes away mysteriously, and Meg's father goes away mysteriously. And Frodo tries to figure out how he goes away in a different manner than Meg.

73

Dana: She kind of related to me like Charlie Brown because Charlie from Charlie
           Brown is kind of like Meg because he's quiet and shy and . . . but . . . Meg's
           not as shy. He's kind of like Charles Wallace instead. And Meg's kind of
           like Lucy where she's not afraid to say something and she wants to say it.
Tiana: I kind of think Charles Wallace is like one of those scary movies when
           there's a kid in this haunted house . . .

The discourse of the young women in this girl power group indicates they are establishing themselves as insiders into literature, using their prior knowledge of popular culture as important background knowledge to flesh out characters. They gently correct members when their interpretations seem off. Tiana, a quiet member, tends to speak last, but she is able to show her interpretations of text, allowing Charles Wallace to be associated with a scary mood, demonstrating that she connects affectively with a character.

> Pedagogical Insight #8: "Going deep" so that students use literature to discuss inequities in society is complicated and often needs several personal and textual examples to convince others of one's claims. Social injustice in the lives of adolescents may also be messier and look different than a teacher's view of social injustice.

When the girl power groups lead a whole-class discussion, the young women use *A Wrinkle in Time* to address social injustice.

One member poses a difficult question that immediately pits males against females: Why are women looked down on by men in the workplace and in politics? The question is followed by a long silence. Caroline is uncomfortable with silence.

Caroline: Come on, throw her a bone.
Indigo: We're going to have to call on you guys.
Matt: Give them a second to think about it. [Lengthy silence ensues.]

A male student asks the girl power group what they think, a clever way of dodging the question. The groups insist they do not want to answer the question without discussion first. The same male student asks Matt what he thinks. Matt says he wants to know what the class thinks. Finally, a female student observes it's been that way since George Washington when girls weren't able to go to school.

In hindsight, we think that had Caroline and her group been instructed to provide a case that first proves that "women are looked down on by men in the workplace and politics," students would have some prior knowledge to respond to as part of the discussion. But although the discussion flounders at first, Caroline has an original interpretation to make about the historical lack of respect for the traditional private work of women versus public work outside the home. Other young women contest her point, making Caroline's initial feminist point more complex.

Caroline: My little comment about it is that oftentimes women are put into the matronly or motherly role, so that means it was often seen as weaker because they wouldn't have to go out and do stuff like . . . uh . . . go run the shop or work on the farm as much, so they wouldn't be seen as strong.
Indigo: Some people think that staying home all the time is a harder job than working.
Caroline: Uh huh.
Chelle: Try raising three kids or more than that.
Caroline: Try raising a kid or two.
Chelle: Yah! When your husband's always working!

Chelle has subtly amended Caroline's views. A good discussion is starting in which new learning is becoming visible. As the girl power group has noted, strong girls and women are not defined by employment outside the home; working at home can demonstrate strength as well.

Group members then ask if Meg can be considered a strong girl character or a character reliant on other characters.

Nolan: Well, I've been kind of reading it and I don't know. I don't see her kind very often because to me she seems like she's kind of going along with the crowd in a way. Like she's not doing much right now.

A male student notes that Meg likes to hold Calvin's hand for guidance. A female student observes so far in the book she seems like she's in a daze and is uncertain of what she is supposed to do. Although Meg finds her girl power later in the book when she is willing to risk her life to save her brother, the girl power group is asking students to engage in feminist thinking that positions characters as more or less powerful depending on the choices they can make for themselves and those they care about.

 Pedagogical Insight #9: Examples of social injustice claims from pop culture can be useful knowledge that can support literacy claims. Media images particularly enhance discussion.

The girl power group shows the class PowerPoint slides of female celebrity images they have collected. They have an important point to make about female dress and want to use diverse media to analyze their main idea. Various slides present supporting details that dress can undermine a woman's intellectual and physical power. The first slide shows an early image of Catwoman.

Caroline: So you can see the outfit she is wearing is very modest and very nice, and it shows that she's a really strong female character according to the trailers and stuff. And I think she'll be a good character in the movies.

The next slide is of Angelina Jolie. Several students call out her name when the slide appears.

Caroline: This is another character. It shows that sometimes movie heroes, technically the female ones, oftentimes they'll try to exemplify some of the traits or . . .
Student: The short shorts!
Caroline: Yah, the short shorts. You can't see it very well because of the title, but there are very, very short shorts.

> Pedagogical Insight #10: Let students choose the images for discussion. Sometimes teachers unnecessarily sanitize images and, in so doing, detract from potential student engagement, the most important characteristic of lively literature discussion.

Caroline wants to make a point that revealing clothes might, at times, diminish the power of women and girls if the embodiment choices of a character visually override the intellectual or heroic qualities of the human being inside the physical "package." So she shows a slide of the character Katniss from *The Hunger Games*.

Caroline: So this is Katniss Everdeen in *The Hunger Games*, and I can't find a full body shot, but her outfit's just a pair of jeans and a shirt and jacket.
Indigo: [Pointing] Kind of like [female student's] pants.
Chelle: It's pretty modest.
Caroline: It's nice and modest and it's realistic.

Noting how similar Katniss's dress is to a female student's, the girl power group observes that realistic dress helps the spirit of a girl shine through the physical house of the girl. The next slide is of the Black Widow.

Caroline: And this next slide is kind of . . . This is Black Widow from the *Avengers* and *Ironman 2*. It's purple. She's wearing just basically a leather suit that's just skin tight and it's . . .
Indigo: Not modest.

The next slide is of Halle Berry as Catwoman. Caroline uses the last two images to introduce a new concept: objectification of women in which the attractive physical body becomes the most defining characteristic for females.

Caroline: And this next one is basically [there is a lot of noise in reaction to the photograph] . . . It's a glorified bikini from a back-then movie. [Caroline continues to talk but it's hard to hear because of student reaction and comments.] And that's all of our PowerPoint. [Students clap.]

Mr. A: Why don't we have a couple of you pull up chairs [in the middle of the circle of desks] so that you can lead the discussion?

Caroline: Okay, based on the slide show and pictures that we showed you, we're going to talk about the objectification, I think is the correct way to say it, of women in movies. So you can see that it's . . .

Mr. A: What does that mean . . . "objectification"?

Caroline: Like they're saying that mostly women are just there to look pretty . . . and . . .

Student: Eye candy.

Caroline: Yah, eye candy.

Indigo: Even, like, the Batman.

Caroline: Catwoman. Even though they may not be the main character, they're still going to be dressed up like eye candy to get people to see it.

A good discussion in which students are making claims and justifying based on evidence from popular culture is occurring. But, what you cannot tell from the vignettes of student talk is that the class is engaged and wants to say more about the images they have just witnessed. This is like silent applause that a discussion is going well. At this point, hands should not have to be raised in order to contribute as long as people are not speaking over each other. In the next conversational turn, Indigo introduces a reason that scantily clad women are often seen in movies. She uses a media image to clarify the salient point her group is trying to make. Caroline observes the absurdity of an action hero wearing a bikini, a garment not conducive to crime fighting.

Indigo: To get more people to come to it.

Caroline: When the characters themselves it might not be realistic for them to wear, like Catwoman, a glorified bikini.

Indigo: How do you guys feel about how women are objectified in movies? Neo? [His hand is up.]

Neo: I think it's not the case in most movies. Except a few. [This is followed by laughter and expressions of disbelief. A student says "Wow," indicating that Neo's conversational turn is naive.]

Chase: That they're okay with that. Showing off their "traits" as you said and with that they, like, get paid and everything but it's pretty much just showing off them—not adapting to the movie.

Indigo: Okay.

Mr. A: Isn't this just a kind of a movie?

Chase: Yeah.

Mr. A: So if you're watching movies meant for older people, you might tend to see more of the Catwoman-type outfits because they would attract men to come see them. [Laughter.]

Indigo: Even the new *Avengers* movie. Black Widow. Skin-tight clothes.

Neo has an unpopular rebuttal that he continues trying to make in the next vignette. He seems to be saying that perhaps revealing clothes on women are a tool to reveal the setting of a story and the cultural values of characters in a storyline. They may serve a purpose in making the plot realistic:

Neo: Like movies like *Burlesque* or like the TV show *Smash*—it's about women, but they're not objectifying women because—[some girls disagree loudly] No! It's about, they're talking about Broadway and there's not really much objectification about it.

His peers disagree.

Harry: Like most movies, that's probably what's going to make them watch it. Like *Twilight* stuff. Cuz Taylor Lautner—cuz all people watch it. [There is a lot of chatter about whether boys and men can be objectified too.]

Chelle: Does that make it okay for girls to watch it?

Caroline: It doesn't make it okay for girls to do it, even though . . .

Indigo: When Taylor Lautner takes off his shirt! [The chatter resumes.]

Male student: Every five seconds!

Caroline: An interesting statistic that I found is that most directors are in fact male, and they're the ones that make most of the big decisions like costumes and stuff.

Mr. A: If they're wearing skimpy clothes, why does that mean they're objectified?

Caroline: Because oftentimes they'll wear the skimpy clothes just so that guys can . . . It's a ploy to get people to watch.

This conversation is a useful one for deeper understanding of the aesthetics of the human form: Is a state of undress in visual media a ploy for men to watch a movie (after all, most directors are men, as Caroline's research has revealed), or can it make an important statement about humanity? (The nudity in *Schindler's List*, for example, is not meant to be titillating but, rather, exposes humankind's inhumanity.) Lack of clothing in high art can be a tool to showcase the beauty and line of the human body. Why not in popular culture also, at least sometimes?

Adding a new twist to Caroline's argument that women are objectified so that men will view a movie, Harry observes that males can be objectified as well as females, and that too can be dehumanizing. As Chelle observes, it is as wrong for males to be objectified as it is for females. Everyone is more than a body.

Did the Girl Power Group Meet Matt's Learning Targets?

When Matt planned this unit, he had several learning targets, which are included in his first week of lesson plans presented at the end of this chapter:

- **SL.7.1.** Come to discussions prepared, having read or researched the material under study; explicitly draw on that preparation by referring to evidence on the topic, text, or issue to probe and reflect on ideas under discussion.

- **SL.7.1.** Follow rules for collegial discussions, track progress toward specific goals and deadlines, and define individual roles as needed.

- **RL.7.1.** Cite several pieces of textual evidence to support analysis of what the text says explicitly as well as inferences drawn from the text.

- **SL.7.1.** Engage effectively in a range of collaborative discussions (one-on-one, in groups, and teacher-led) with diverse partners on grade 7 topics, texts, and issues, building on others' ideas and expressing their own clearly.

  o Pose questions that elicit elaboration and respond to others' questions and comments with relevant observations and ideas that bring the discussion back on topic as needed.

  o Acknowledge new information expressed by others and, when warranted, modify their own views.

- **SL.7.2.** Analyze the main ideas and supporting details presented in diverse media and formats (e.g., visually, quantitatively, orally) and explain how the ideas clarify a topic, text, or issue under study.

- **RL.7.2.** Determine a theme or central idea of a text and analyze its development over the course of the text; provide an objective summary of the text.

- **RL.7.4a.** Determine the meaning of words and phrases as they are used in a text, including figurative and connotative meanings.

- **RL.7.6.** Analyze how an author develops and contrasts the points of view of different characters or narrators in a text.

Were these learning targets met using evidence from student voices presented in this chapter? The transcripts of the girl power groups indicate they were. The young women prepared and led a half-hour discussion in which peers constructed new knowledge about the role of women in society (SL.7.1). They brought in diverse media to present and clarify an important point about how female dress can objectify women (and male dress, or lack of it, can objectify men at times) (SL.7.2). They demonstrated how a feminist lens can pull certain themes from a text (SL.7.2). And they presented several points of view in interpreting the character of Meg (SL.7.6).

Assessing Discussion

Assuming that most teachers will not often use video to capture student voices as evidence of met learning targets as we did, other assessment tools can assist teachers in demonstrating that students are working to meet speaking and listening learning targets. Measuring speaking and listening targets through student talk is problematic. Unlike traditional written assessment, which can be more easily quantified, student talk can disappear forever into a sea of vague echoes. There are ways, however, for students and teachers to recognize that learning has occurred during discussions. In response to the vagaries of assessing discussion, Matt developed rubrics for speaking and listening.

Because students were to read assigned passages of texts and think about discussions in advance by annotating their reading with what they found interesting or confusing, connections with passages and real life, and words they found confusing, students came to discussions with some preparation and an organic organization to small groups. The varied connections students made with various characters in *A Wrinkle in Time* showed that they were prepared to participate in discussion.

Matt created small-group and whole-class rubrics, which he placed on a clipboard as he observed students engage in small-group discussions.

For small and large groups, Matt established criteria that helped him assess the quality of discussion. When he sat with small groups, he noted whether students were backing their textual claims with evidence (Standard 7.1), correctly summarizing textual themes (Standard 7.2), and addressing challenging vocabulary (7.4a). These criteria became the rules for small-group discussion: (1) If you make a claim, summarize the passage you are referring to; (2) back your textual claims with evidence (using page numbers to refer back to in order to read aloud your evidence to the group); (3) do not let your connection wander too far off text; (4) using the context surrounding unfamiliar words, discuss the meaning of new words that you think might be important to the passage. Matt's chart is shown in Figure 5.2.

Matt also developed a rubric (Figure 5.3) so that he could evaluate members of whole-class discussions. Before whole-class student-led discussions commenced, he

Student comments show a high-level of comprehension because they are backing their claims with textual evidence.	Name of Student	Yes	No
Student comments are relevant, stay with the text, and do not wander off track.		Yes	No
Student is able to summarize the passage.		Yes	No
Students are identifying elements within the novel when appropriate (emphasizing plot).		Yes	No
Students are using context clues to understand challenging words and passages.		Yes	No
Students are making connections between the novel and prior knowledge.		Yes	No

Figure 5.2 Small-group discussion assessment.

Group Member Name: _____

- He/she clearly read the assigned chapters. __ Agree __ Sort of __ Disagree
- He/she helped to plan the discussion by adding ideas and questions. __ Agree __ Sort of __ Disagree
- He/she was prepared to help lead the discussion. __ Agree __ Sort of __ Disagree
- He/she asked most or all of his/her questions during the discussion. __ Agree __ Sort of __ Disagree
- His/her questions made the discussion better. __ Agree __ Sort of __ Disagree

COMMENTS:
_____
_____

Figure 5.3 Whole-class discussion planning.

participated in planning sessions where students brainstormed the topics they would present, the questions they would ask the class, and the order of questions that might work best. He evaluated students during this planning session using the rubric in Figure 5.3. This rubric works well when assessing whether learning targets of 7.1 have been met.

Finally, Matt asked the class to evaluate the success of each whole-class discussion, an exercise meant to measure the success of targets 7.1 and 7.2 (Figure 5.4). His full lesson plans are shown in Figure 5.5.

Evaluate the following aspects of the discussion on a scale from 1 (disagree) to 10 (agree). Circle your choice.

The topic was interesting.

| 1 | 2 | 3 | 4 | 5 | 6 | 7 | 8 | 9 | 10 |

The leaders asked good
discussion questions (Why, how, what do you think . . .).

| 1 | 2 | 3 | 4 | 5 | 6 | 7 | 8 | 9 | 10 |

The leaders were prepared
with enough questions to fill
the 30 minutes.

| 1 | 2 | 3 | 4 | 5 | 6 | 7 | 8 | 9 | 10 |

The leaders connected the topic
to the novel.

| 1 | 2 | 3 | 4 | 5 | 6 | 7 | 8 | 9 | 10 |

Comments/suggestions:

_____

_____

Figure 5.4 Discussion evaluation.

Note: Discussion elements are shaded.

COMMON CORE STANDARDS MET IN THIS LESSON:

DATE	Monday 4/16/12
LEARNING TARGETS BASED ON COMMON CORE	**SL.7.1. Follow rules for collegial discussions, track progress toward specific goals and deadlines, and define individual roles as needed.** **RL.7.4a. Determine the meaning of words and phrases as they are used in a text, including figurative and connotative meanings.**
BIG QUESTION(S)	• Introduce all questions: (1) What is popular culture? (2) What aspects of popular culture appeal to you? (3) What is the connection between popular culture and *A Wrinkle in Time*? (4) What can characters in *A Wrinkle in Time* learn from what we know from popular culture?
ACTIVITIES	1. Split into "Interest Groups" 2. Introduce Dr. Gritter; explain project; more releases? 3. Explain interest groups and mixed groups 4. Warm up/Book check out

Figure 5.5 Matt's lesson plans for the first week of the unit.

ACTIVITIES	• Book check out
	—Interest group discussion: Each week, we will focus on a specific area within pop culture (sports, music, movies, etc.). There will be one small group in charge of leading a whole-class discussion about that topic. Those small groups are called "interest groups." Group members were placed in an area that would appeal to their interests and background knowledge. For day 3 of the first week, the topic for our whole-class discussion was sports. My expectations for the discussion leaders were: that they begin the discussion by making a connection between the topic and the book (Calvin plays basketball; Sandy and Dennys are "normal" and excel at sports); that they prepare questions and facts to talk about contemporary issues and figures in sports; that they lead the 15–20 minute discussion without teacher interference.
—Tri-Bond game: This is based on the Tri-Bond board game. There is a card with three items on it, and those items share one common link. Instead of using the board game cards (which are a bit tricky for 7th graders), I made some up and put them on PowerPoint slides (EX: Arches; Gate Bridge; Tate: Things that are GOLDEN. Golden Tate is a football player on the Seattle Seahawks). We used it as a warm up activity to get the students thinking about connections. The rest of the unit was based on making connections between pop culture and the novel *A Wrinkle In Time*.
5. Unit Introduction
• *A Wrinkle In Time* at 50
• Individual/group preview of the book
• 1962 vs. 2012
• Explain unit and introduce big questions.
6. How to annotate while reading: I ask the students to annotate for a few reasons. First, I wanted them to read actively. As artificial as it may have been, forcing them to annotate as they read forces them at least think a little bit. Second, I wanted them to have a record of their thoughts for discussion times. Their annotations helped start and guide their discussions of the novel. Finally, I wanted the students to use their annotation for literary analysis. The summative assignment for this unit was a literary analysis essay, and the students used their annotations to support their assertions. As far as what I asked them to do, I asked them to make note of a few things as they read: major questions they had about the story; connections between the story and their own lives; and connections between the story and pop culture. I frequently prompted them to start annotations with "This reminds me of . . ." and "That

(Continued)

ACTIVITIES	is just like . . .". When it came time to write the essays, the students had a good bank of thoughts to begin with and plenty of textual evidence to support their thoughts. Week 1 = sticky notes can be used for annotation. Introduce and write down vocabulary words for the week: content 7; subnormal 9; exclusive 11; prodigious 11; repulsive 13; cunning 19 • Write down words. • Review context clues. • Review adjectives. **Get up, move around game 7. Begin chapter 1 together through page 7; think-aloud annotations • Uncover characters on the wall as introduced. 8. Individual reading and annotation time • Pauses to check and compare annotations 9. Wrap up **HW: Finish chapter 1. Week 1 discussion leaders should get through chapter 2.
PREP/MATERIALS NEEDED	Groups made, novels set aside in library, PPT warm-up, unit intro, sticky notes/bookmarks/notepads . . . WALL DECORATION > character pictures (covered), vocab words (1–3)
ASSESSMENT	Participation for Tri-Bond game

REFLECTION: _____

_____

_____

_____

_____

DATE	Tuesday 4/17/12
LEARNING TARGETS BASED ON COMMON CORE	**SL.7.1. Come to discussions prepared, having read or researched material under study; explicitly draw on that preparation by referring to evidence on the topic, text, or issue to probe and reflect on ideas under discussion.** **RL.7.1. Cite several pieces of textual evidence to support analysis of what the text says explicitly as well as inferences drawn from the text.**
BIG QUESTION(S)	• What is pop culture? • What parts of pop culture appeal to you?
ACTIVITIES	1. Computer Lab (bring book) – Yahoo Sports Minute – Define pop culture, surf and find examples **BIG QUESTIONS – Pinterest introduction/ pages for *AWIT* characters – Find and pin activity

ACTIVITIES	2. Mixed group review
	– Discuss chapter 1. Use/discuss annotations.
	– Discuss a pop culture connection.
	Character Discussion (10)
	– Meg, Mrs. Murray, Charles Wallace, Mrs. Which
	– Place vocabulary words; add other adjectives.
	– Make photo stickers; place and explain.
	3. Read chapter 2/Discussion leader prep (20)
	4. Wrap up
	**HW: Finish chapter 2. Discussion leaders should finish chapter 3.
PREP/MATERIALS NEEDED	Pop culture websites and question sheet, Pinterest boards ready, discussion questions ready, photo pins
ASSESSMENT	Mixed Group Discussion Assessment

REFLECTION: _____
_____
_____
_____
_____

Pop Culture Websites
www.teenvogue.com
www.nick.com
www.kidzworld.com
www.sikids.com
www.timeforkids.com
www.channelone.com

DATE	Wednesday 4/18/12
LEARNING TARGETS BASED ON COMMON CORE	**SL.7.2. Analyze the main ideas and supporting details presented in diverse media and formats (e.g., visually, quantitatively, orally) and explain how the ideas clarify a topic, text, or issue under study.**
	RL.7.6. Analyze how an author develops and contrasts the points of view of different characters or narrators in a text.
BIG QUESTION(S)	• What is pop culture?
	• What parts of pop culture appeal to you?
	• What's the connection between _____ and _____?
ACTIVITIES	1. Yahoo Sports Minute
	**BIG QUESTION 1
	2. Warm up: Principal's office video and whole class discussion (10)
	– Connect to chapter 2
	3. Mixed groups review
	– Discuss chapter 2 using annotations.
	– Discuss a pop culture connection.
	**BIG QUESTION 2

(Continued)

ACTIVITIES	– Vocabulary: antagonistic 27; plump 35
	– Freeze frame activity using chapters 1 and 2
	4. Character Discussion
	– Update vocabulary and adjectives.
	– New characters: Calvin; Mrs. Who
	**BIG QUESTION 3
	5. Demonstrate tomorrow's whole class discussion
	– Expectations
	– Leader evaluations
	6. Read chapter 3/Discussion leader prep
	7. Wrap up
	**HW: Finish chapter 3 (quiz tomorrow). Discussion leaders prepare the discussion for tomorrow.
PREP/MATERIALS NEEDED	Principal's office video; Discussion questions ready; rubric for discussion evaluations
ASSESSMENT	Mixed Group Discussion Assessment Freeze Frame Activity

REFLECTION: _____

_____

_____

_____

_____

DATE	Thursday 4/19/12
LEARNING TARGETS BASED ON COMMON CORE	**SL.7.1. Engage effectively in a range of collaborative discussions (one-on-one, in groups, and teacher-led) with diverse partners on grade 7 topics, texts, and issues, building on others' ideas and expressing their own clearly.**
	Pose questions that elicit elaboration and respond to others' questions and comments with relevant observations and ideas that bring the discussion back on topic as needed. Acknowledge new information expressed by others and, when warranted, modify their own views.
	RL.7.6. Analyze how an author develops and contrasts the points of view of different characters or narrators in a text.
BIG QUESTION(S)	• What parts of pop culture appeal to you?
	• What's the connection between _____ and _____?
ACTIVITIES	1. Warm up: Yahoo Sports Minute + journal for discussion: Since not all students are aware of what is going on in the world of sports, the *Yahoo Sports Minute* clips provided a short, quick-hitting recap of popular stories in sports for the day. That way, come discussion time, everyone had at least a little bit of prior knowledge about the topic.
	2. Mixed groups review
	– Discuss chapter 3 using annotations.
	– Discuss warm-up journal
	– Vocabulary: sullen 43; classified 50 (no big group)

ACTIVITIES	3. Quiz: Chapters 1–3
	4. Big group discussion
	  – Intro Activity
	  – Discussion
	5. Interest groups discussion
	  – Big group discussion evaluation
	  – Brainstorm ideas for future discussion.
	6. Vocabulary review game
	  – Review all words.
	  – Game
	7. Wrap up
	  **HW: Vocabulary quiz tomorrow. Annotations completed for chapters 1–3.

PREP/MATERIALS NEEDED	Quiz and copies, big group discussion prep, evaluation sheets and copies, Pictionary slips
ASSESSMENT	Participation Quiz Leader Evaluation for Big Group Discussion. Discussion Evaluation for Class

REFLECTION: _____
_____
_____
_____
_____

DATE	Friday 4/20/12
LEARNING TARGETS BASED ON COMMON CORE	**SL.7.2. Analyze the main ideas and supporting details presented in diverse media and formats (e.g., visually, quantitatively, orally) and explain how the ideas clarify a topic, text, or issue under study.** **RL.7.2. Determine a theme or central idea of a text and analyze its development over the course of the text; provide an objective summary of the text.**
BIG QUESTION(S)	• What parts of pop culture appeal to you? • What's the connection between _____ and _____?

ACTIVITIES	1. Vocabulary quiz and annotations
	2. Warm-up
	3. Verb tense emphasizing passages in text where tenses changed
	  – Notes
	  – Guided practice – book predictions
	4. Mixed group discussion: Television portrayal of fathers
	  – Reading
	  – Class brainstorm of TV fathers
	  – Whole-class discussion of Mr. Murray
	  – Mixed group discussion
	5. The week in review: Q & A to check for student understanding and recall of the skills and concepts we learned. Will include week's vocabulary (and the use of context clues), how to annotate, and verb tense.

(Continued)

PREP/MATERIALS NEEDED	Quiz and copies, notes prepared, "TV Dads" copies, discussion questions ready
ASSESSMENT	Mixed Group Discussion Assessment Quiz Annotations

REFLECTION: _____

_____

_____

_____

_____

The combination of evidence from video vignettes and hard copy rubrics provided us with satisfactory evidence that the literary reading of Matt's students was becoming more sophisticated over time. His students demonstrate strong interpretive skills, which they showcase in front of peers and teachers. They construct new knowledge as they speak to each other. Most are motivated to speak about their new learning and are deeply engaged in a common literary text. They are in the process of becoming college and career ready. And that is the point of a curriculum tailored to the Common Core State Standards.

Opportunity for Reflection

Consider how you might apply the ideas from this chapter to your own classroom.

1. Reflect for a moment on a passage from literature you teach that is especially poignant for you because of the personal connections you can make with it. Share your story with a class and deliberately connect your experience with literature. Cover the same literary passage with another class but refrain from telling your story. Can students from the first class recall your story in a few days' time? Can they recall the literary passage you connected it to? Can the second class recall the literary passage?

2. Has a student shared a personal story that could become a valuable literary bridge? Will students let you share their personal stories? Why or why not? Can students recall the story later in the unit? Can they recall the literary passage it was connected to?

3. Do adolescents pay more attention to controversial texts than to safe texts? Why or why not?

4. How can you set purposes for student independent or class reading of literature that sets up opportunities for livelier class discussion?

5. After perusing speaking and listening Common Core standards, what are the discussion strengths of your classes? What are discussion needs that should become learning targets?

6. Compare student writing when discussion was a pre-writing activity versus "cold" writing in which students had to write without discussion (such as for a high-stakes state writing test). Which activity yielded more conceptually rich writing? Why is this the case?

7. Have you taught students the explicit vocabulary of making arguments: stating a claim, offering evidence, knowing the difference between warranted and unwarranted claims, the importance of counterexamples, logical fallacies? Do you use this language of argument during your discussions? How does knowing the genre of argument lead to tighter discussion?

8. Reflect on a student discussion that "went deep." What were the conditions of depth of discussion?

9. How have students used popular culture references to illuminate textual passages? Under what discussions can popular culture references distract from literature learning? What are techniques that bring discussion back to literary analysis?

10. What stories from popular culture are students talking about? Can these stories be used as bridges in the literature you are scheduled to teach this year? How can you set up permeable connections to literature?

11. Peruse Matt's full lesson plans for the first week of a unit (Figure 5.5). Is this good planning? Why or why not? Do his learning targets, big questions, activities, and assessments work together? Select a particular learning target from the first day of class and trace how it culminates in ethical assessment, where what students have learned in class and homework is eventually measured the first week or could be measured in following weeks.

6

Successful Discussions and Classroom Democracy in Action

In this chapter we want to show how student access to popular culture can enhance literary understanding evidenced in discussions while meeting Common Core State Standards for literary reading. Connections students made among superheroes, modern-day heroes, and characters and events in *A Wrinkle in Time* enticed Matt's students into examination of cultural heroes and superheroes and what they mean in the world they live in. Matt is borrowing from Cawelti's view of popular culture as reflecting, expressing, and reinforcing societal values. In his classroom, superheroes, a subset of popular culture, become a common language for students to analyze a canonical text.

The following vignettes of classroom talk demonstrate rich discussion that shows classroom democracy in action and preparation for the many skills required for democracy to flourish: stating what one thinks and providing evidence for claims, active listening to the ideas of others, and attempting to come to some kind of consensus within a group while allowing disagreement. Students facilitating the superhero discussions presented in this chapter get to have a literal say in what their class will discuss and, therefore, learn. Such curricular organization is precisely what it takes to train future leaders to participate in democracy. Like the last chapter, we will include our pedagogical insights for using popular culture as a gateway into literature through student discussion. They will be generally followed by anchor standards for literary reading.

Vignettes of Class Discussions

In the first vignettes of discussion, students placed in a superheroes group borrow a strategy that the sports group has already used in a previous discussion in which classmates were asked to participate in a public opinion poll. In the first transcript presented below, students plan for how they will set up their discussion; in the second, we see that their planning has paid off: Peers want to talk about connections of superheroes and characters in *A Wrinkle in Time*.

In the first discussion, a group member has already decided that a good way to introduce the discussion is for characters to make a list of superheroes and to decide who is the "superest" superhero of them all. This planning activity is in keeping with the anchor standard for reading literature 7.7: Compare written literature with film, plays, and multimedia by analyzing similarities and differences in artistic techniques across media.

As the rest of the class is reading the day's chapter silently, Matt walks over to the "superheroes" group to check in with their plans for the whole-class discussion they will lead:

Nolan: We already have a game so far.

Mr. A: What's the game about? [The student who came up with the hook to start the discussion explains it to Matt. He nods his head.] The superchampion? Do you have brackets? Okay. So that will get them going. And then your goal after that? Yeah? I like that game idea. I think it's good. So then that should take fivish minutes or so, which leaves twenty to twenty-five for the rest. Now I've told all the other groups this: The ideal way for you to do this is for you to come in with questions for you to ask and then sit back and watch what you've created so students can discuss the good ideas that you have. Okay? So if you are doing an excellent job, you shouldn't be talking too much. You should be posting really good questions and then listening, and when discussion starts to die off a little bit, you go in with your next good question. All right? So what kinds of things about heroes, about the story, or connections between the two do you think they'd want to talk about?

Nolan: Would they have finished the book by then?

Mr. A: They should. Yeah.

Nolan: Okay. So we can't have any questions like "Who is going to win in the end?" So those are out.

Mr. A: Well, that's not a great discussion. Can you think of a way to add a why or a how to that?

> Pedagogical Insight #1: Do instruct students how to set up discussion so they can facilitate it themselves, like they will have to do for most of their lives. First, students need to know that there are different kinds of questions. Questions with yes or no responses generally result in recitation. Open-ended questions encourage students to cite textual evidence to support claims (RL.7.1).

Joel: I was thinking why something about Mr. Murray. Like, why [he did] something he did. Like Meg thought it was bad that he tested Charles Wallace.

Mr. A: Do you consider him to be a hero in the story?

Joel: Yeah, because he's kind of heroic. He's kind of like a good leader and he saves people from IT.

Mr. A: Okay, so might it be a good thing for them to talk about who in the story might be considered a hero? Which of the characters and why?

Joel: Yeah.

Mr. A: You could think about that with what about the bad things that he did or things that are questionable—and is that normal for heroes? What about if that's your thing to lead? Who in this book is a hero? Why are they a hero? Are they still a hero if they do things that we would say are bad? Nolan, can you help him with that, so it could be a job for you two guys?

Nolan: Maybe I could remind them that most superheroes have a downfall. Like, what's their weakness? Like most stories you watch, like *Superman* has a time when he's not doing that great in the movie. Like is there a part in the movie when they're not doing that great?

Mr. A: Compared to the story?

Nolan: Yeah.

Mr. A: With more than one character I'm assuming from the story?

Nolan: Yeah.

Mr. A: Okay, that can be your part following Joel. What else?

> Pedagogical Insight #2: When students are to lead a discussion, assign members to present their open-ended questions in writing after they have brainstormed questions with all members in their group. Good questions are the basis of a good discussion.

> Pedagogical Insight #3: Assigning popular culture themes to groups helps them ask good questions. Note how Nolan's existing repertoire of superhero knowledge allows him a framework to compare and contrast points of view of characters in a text (RL.7.6). His knowledge of the fatal flaw of Superman may help other students understand the complexity of literary characters like Mr. Murray. It is important knowledge some teachers might overlook depending on their views of popular culture.

A group member wants to lead a discussion on what would have happened if Meg had been unable to summon love for Charles Wallace and defeat the enemy.

Mr. A: Okay, so it's the issue of love versus hate. Okay, use that as an example to lead into that [discussion], but do you think that's a common theme throughout the genre about heroes?

The superheroes group think that superhero stories do tend to be about love versus hate. They seem to have arrived at a generative theme for a rich discussion.

Mr. A: Okay, so maybe you can make the connection between this story and love versus hate, light versus dark, good versus evil. Are there other stories or movies where you see the same thing? Do you remember the part of the story when they are talking about the people who fought for the light? [The group members nod.] And they list all those famous people? Jesus, Beethoven, Bach. Do you remember why they listed all those people?

Joel: I think because they were wondering how those people defeated the darkness.

Mr. A: So if those people are heroes against the dark, what does that tell you about the dark? What is the dark according to this book?

Joel: Failure and defeat, basically. Or something like that.

Mr. A: Why those people?

Joel: Because they were great and smart . . .

Mr. A: Smart?

Joel: Intelligent.

Mr. A: Da Vinci?

Joel: Inventive. Creative.

Mr. A: So what does that tell you? If those things are the light? What is the dark?

Joel: Destructive. Uh, stupid.

Mr. A: What was Camazotz like?

Joel: Uh, just plain. There's nothing really there.

Mr. A: So the lack of creativity, the lack of thought.

Joel: Everything was the same for the entire city.

> Pedagogical Insight #4: Encourage students to grapple with features of story grammar (characters, setting, dialogue, conflict, resolution) to make cause and effect statements (RL.7.2). Matt's expert questioning in the small group allows the superhero group to see a major theme of the book. They can now break down this theme with their peers when they lead in questioning later.

Love, creativity, and light are the essence of superheroes, the group decides, as Matt masterfully but subtly leads them to this conclusion through open-ended questions and some textual reminders. Hate, conformity, and darkness are the essence of villains. The setting of Camazotz, where all characters must behave the same, allows evil to flourish. This might be a metaphor to allow classmates to consider the differences in literary characters and superheroes and villains.

This small-group discussion was an important scaffold for the class discussion a week later. The superheroes group uses Matt's feedback, and a generative discussion ensues.

The following vignette shows that this group was able to turn their planning into a rich whole-class discussion in which the class interprets the weaknesses of characters in *A Wrinkle in Time* and the weaknesses of superheroes. Nolan begins by leading the class discussion.

Nolan: Just like Superman had his Kryptonite, do you think, like, in the story, Meg and Charles have some weakness? Neo?

Neo: I think their weakness is fear of what could happen to their father.

Nolan: James?

James: I think Meg's weakness is Charles because she likes him so much and she would do anything for him.

Although Nolan could build more ably on Neo's response, the discussion is already going someplace interesting. As James notes, sometimes love is not a strength. Loving too much might also be a weakness because it might interfere with one's own rights or the rights of a collective group. The class discussion continues:

Chelle: Charles's weakness is probably physical strength. Like, he doesn't seem very physically strong, as opposed to Meg, who's constantly getting in fights. . . . So Charles's [weakness] would be, like, if someone were to beat him up.

Neo, a nonconformist (he is in the music group), has an original point to make.

Neo: I think another weakness for the people is their willpower.

Students: What? [This turn doesn't seem to make sense to a few students.]

Neo defends his point with textual evidence.

Neo: Because the superheroes we were mentioning, their strength is their will to fight. And Meg and Charles Wallace's will doesn't seem as strong. Because that's why Charles got hypnotized.

Nolan: Do you think the other side, the bad side, has weaknesses?

Harry: Well, like, IT has the weakness from love.

Neo: I just have to say that every villain has a weakness because villains do things because of the things that have happened to them and they feel like they need to take revenge on the things that have happened to them and that they're scared and frightened. And they want revenge to make everybody else feel like that. That's why they become villains.

Chelle: IT must have a weakness because he was beat by Meg. So if he were immortal and didn't have a weakness, then obviously she would not have been able to beat him.

Neo: Oh, and another thing. Just to add to my point that villains do things because someone makes fun of them, that's why they become a villain. For Batman . . . I mean the Riddler. He became the Riddler because of people making fun of his ideas. And that's why he became evil and stuff.

Students are having Reader Response reactions to their classroom text as they bring in multiple interpretations of their knowledge of superheroes, including Neo, who is trying to consider the sense-making of villains. We can also see reading comprehension as sense-making of interpersonal relationships. Although students do not agree with Neo's first claim that the good characters lack willpower, he feels comfortable to explore his startling claim and to make new points about villains. Disagreeing for a moment with the premise of the book that "good guys" don't have the same willpower as villains, he cites as evidence the character of Charles Wallace, who managed to get himself hypnotized because he was weak. James introduces a novel idea: Loving "too much" might be construed to be a weakness. Chelle's remark is particularly astute. In the next book in L'Engle's series, *A Wind in the Door*, Charles Wallace's degenerating health provides the central plot; there is foreshadowing in this book, the prequel. Nolan's final question is generative for Harry and Chelle and allows Neo to complete his line of thought. Villains, in fact, have willpower often fueled by revenge. Making fun of people and their ideas changes people and has consequences. It is an important concept for middle schoolers and for all of us who want to build more humane communities. This leads us to the next Pedagogical Insight.

Pedagogical Insight #5: If you really want students to make inferences so they can read between the lines of a text, they MUST access their prior knowledge of how people (even superheroes) make sense of life events. Encourage this!

Student discourse accomplishes Common Core State Standards in this class discussion for speaking and listening and literary reading. Speakers offer claims and arguments, and listeners evaluate those arguments and the soundness of evidence, although there are times when discussion leaders can be encouraged to ask additional questions to get at this. Students also use examples from text to support their inferences about the motivations of characters.

Pedagogical Insight #6: Embrace textual complexity as being a mirror of the complexity of the world we live in. Questions that embrace human complexity will likely be generative.

In the next vignette, the superheroes group is still facilitating the discussion. The class has identified several characters from *A Wrinkle in Time* and listed them on the board. Characters include Aunt Beast, Meg, Calvin, and Mrs. W. Additional, non-textual forces for good, including "army," are also listed with these characters. After each character, blanks are drawn so that students can come up with foils for good characters. Students are asked to come up with their opposites in the real world. The discussion turns highly metaphorical as students attempt to name good forces and bad forces in the world in which they live. Students contest binaries of good and evil. Figuring out good and evil in the real world, it seems, is hard work.

James: For the dark side, Al-Qaida. [This is followed by a lot of instantaneous student comment.] Well, kind of . . . Why'd you write "army" for the light side?

Caroline: So? There can be an evil army. [This is followed by a lot of instantaneous student comment.] Yah, like the Al-Qaida army.

A group member observes that the army helps us.

Nolan: Like to *you*, to *you*. But a specific group.

Caroline: On the bad side, pop culture. [She mentions a television show that follows celebrity gossip "news."] The reason I say that is because sometimes they have bad things such as [. . .] or more like stupid things like how someone ate breakfast.

Mr. A: Would anyone take the opposite side of [Caroline's] and say pop culture can be light as opposed to dark? [This is followed by a chorus of yesses and no's.] Do you want to explain?

Indigo: Well, like, it doesn't always have to be bad because, like, pop culture just isn't bad. I mean there's other stuff too.

Mr. A: Like what, [Indigo]?

Indigo: Gosh. I'm not thinking.

Mr. A: If we're talking about light and darkness and light being good and dark being bad like in the story, there are some aspects of pop culture that people would consider darkness—but some aspects could you consider to be light and good and helpful and edifying?

Harry: It can be good and can help you. Like, it could be a guy that tells everything about what not to do. [Students break into side chats.]

Mr. A: [Harry], are you talking about a person?

Harry: Yeah. Like there's stuff in magazines if you read. Then if the stuff they say is good, then what's bad is saying, well, you know, you shouldn't do it. [A student observes that a magazine should not determine what is right or wrong.] But if it's in there, it's helping you.

Harry is trying to make the point that sometimes telling the harsh truth about harmful activities can be a good thing. Sometimes people who have done bad things, including celebrities and superheroes, can do a good thing by exposing what they have done wrong by way of warning to others. Matt wants to clarify this point. James wants to make another point: that poverty and war are more the antitheses of good than popular culture that is frivolous.

Mr. A: So you're saying more advice as opposed to right and wrong?

Caroline: Yeah, but some of that stuff can be really frivolous. Like have you ever seen this guy where it says lose five pounds in five weeks. And another one will say lose six pounds in five weeks. But oftentimes they don't really work as well.

James: I think that though pop culture can be bad, it's not on a level of poverty and war. So I don't think we should write it down.

> Pedagogical Insight #7: Side talk on the topic of discussion is applause. Embrace it! Perhaps it would be a good idea for students to slow down the discussion, write down their opinions on the tenor of talk, and share their reasoning.

The intervals of side talk in the vignette above indicates students highly involved in reflecting on good and evil in their world. Students are thinking and rethinking often static notions of good and evil.

Later, Matt asks students if heroes can be bad people. Student responses show mental agility: It depends on whether the hero is acting in a manner that reinforces one's existing ideology. Perceptions of good might rest on prior knowledge of goodness.

Abe: Like a bad group, like a terrorist organization. The people that work for them, they consider the leader their hero.

Indigo: Yeah, well. I guess. If there are two sides going to war or something. Then each side views their commander or leader as the hero. The other side would view that person as not the hero but as evil. I guess it depends on if people are thinking the person is a hero.

Roxy: Usually heroes are somebody who thinks they are doing good and they
           think that they are a hero, but to everyone else they are still a guy.
Cassandra: Like Indigo was saying: It depends on who you agree with.

Here students are responding to each other's comments and keeping discussion
on track by actively listening. Cassandra echoes Indigo's earlier contribution. This conversation echoes the previous conversation. Deciding who is a hero and who is good
might depend on prior perceptions and ideology.

Pedagogical Insight #8: Note recurring discussion themes in your records
(perhaps on giant Post-it Notes on classroom walls) and turn these into unit
foci (essay questions on exams, for example). When students revoice, they
demonstrate they care about a topic. When students care, they are optimally open
for learning. That's the point of literature, we think.

Good guys, villains, and happy endings become recurring motifs in this particular class. Popular culture allows students to collectively voice familiarity with literary
structure and make the text-to-text connections of good readers. In the next vignette,
Jonah wonders why the good guys always win in books. Matt lets the students unravel
their way out of his initial wondering, which leads us to:

Pedagogical Insight #9: Let the students do the heavy thinking about literature. Your job is to set this up. Language arts teachers tend to talk too much!
Notice below how students are analyzing how plots can develop in their
discussion (RL.7.2).

Jonah: I think it's weird that in regular books, unlike the thing at the beginning,
           the good guy always wins. It's like they never have the villain win and
           nothing more, no other sequels.
Mr. A: Would you want to read a book where the bad guy won? [A few students
           say they would actually.]
Louis: What about in *Twilight*? I mean, Edward is sort of the bad guy, and he wins
           with Bella.
Chelle: In King Arthur, everyone dies. Not just the bad guy.
Caroline: It kind of reminds me how sometimes the character doesn't even fight
           with the villain directly but they still defeat the villain. Like, they might
           destroy big weapons people. And if for some reason they didn't continue
           the series, you could always assume the weapons people were so impor-
           tant they had a plot against the whole military.

Nolen:	Well, like in *Romeo and Juliet*. Both of them die. It's kind of a sad story. It's kind of famous for everyone dying.
Mr. A:	It's a tragic ending.
Hal:	In *Monty Python and the Holy Grail*, they don't even finish the thing, they get arrested before they finish. [Big guffaws from a few boys.]
Mr. A:	So it's kind of a silly ending? Do you see kind of a buildup to a bad-guy versus a good-guy ending here in our story that we're reading now? Who's the bad guy?
Ned:	The Man with the Red Eyes.
Mr. A:	The Man with the Red Eyes is controlled by IT, right?—and presumably generates this black cloud, at least in my imagination. So we have bad. Do we have people fighting against bad?

A student wagers a guess that the Man with the Red Eyes is Meg's dad. Matt observes that this is not an unreasonable guess. He notices that the plot is coming to a climax that will end with a resolution. The beauty of this moment is that students are doing most of the talking about literature, initiating comments and questions showing their comprehension and engagement with literature with examples and counterexamples of plot structures (thanks to popular culture). Matt does not need to direct the literary talk but does guide students back to *A Wrinkle in Time*.

> Pedagogical Insight #10: Let it "go deep" (within reason; sometimes student talk can turn into bullying or self-damage). A great literary discussion becomes personal. ELA teachers may not be licensed therapists, but unintentional therapy (or pain) happens in our classrooms every day. Some call this bibliotherapy. If it gets "too deep," you will want to get school counselors involved.

Culminating the superheroes discussion becomes very personal, as students ponder the heroes in their lives and their qualities. It starts with a question posed by Chase, who is leading the discussion.

Chase:	Who's your hero?—and explain why they are your personal hero. So if you would raise your hands, we won't have a bunch of talking.
Indigo:	[Raising hand] My grandpa, because he was also in the Vietnam War. And he was also there for me, and he was there for my mom when my real dad wasn't.
Chase:	Good. Yes?
Brendon:	I'd say my brother . . . because he was a state trooper and now he's coming into Washington, and he's going to other people's houses and doing a lot of scary stuff. And a lot of his friends died already because they did that.

Chase: So he's a state trooper. Is it for Washington?
Brendon: He was in Alaska.
Chase: Alaska. Okay.
Mr. A: Why do you think that armed forces soldiers and law enforcement officers are such common heroes?
Indigo: Because they are sometimes risking their lives because it's dangerous out in the field, and it makes us feel comforted, maybe.

Students culminate this line of discussion by realizing that heroes do not work for their own personal good but sacrifice their lives for others. They are willing to work harder than the average citizen. Many times heroes risk their lives and are not labeled as heroes until they are dead. The conversation goes back to knowledge of superheroes.

> Pedagogical Insight #11: Comparing and contrasting points of views of characters in a text (RL.7.6) is easier when contrasts of accessible characters in popular culture can be made first. Comparing and contrasting is actually pretty hard cognitive work, since they are opposite ways of thinking. It takes a lot of practice, and comparing and contrasting a new story with one that several people have thought about a good deal makes a lot of sense to us.

Chase: If you switched our superheroes with soldiers, how would they be the same, and how would they be different?
Caroline: But the thing about my favorite superhero, Batman . . . [her classmates groan audibly because Caroline is obsessed with Batman and the upcoming movie in recent days] is that he was just an ordinary guy who was given special circumstances that allow him to go out and help people. So that's the same thing as some of the men and women who work in the army. They're in certain circumstances that they want to go out and help.
Adam: So, would the characters be considered heroes or would they be considered superheroes because they could "tesser" [take shortcuts through time and space]?

This conversational turn results in much student talk, the sign that discussion has struck a generative chord. Some students observe that the characters with tessering abilities who helped Meg in journeys across worlds are sidekicks to Meg and do not have the skills to solve her problems. Rather, they assisted her in finding her own way out of the conflicts of the book. Helpful sidekicks can really be heroes!

Cassandra:	Like guardian angels. They don't swoop down and take them but help them.
Ezra:	They didn't save them, they just guided them.
Adam:	In our world today, are we choosing to be like heroes?
Ezra:	Some of us. Some people have celebrities as heroes, and the celebrities don't even care about them.

Ultimately, heroes care about people. If celebrities do not care about people, Ezra concludes, they cannot be heroes. Heroes know right from wrong and choose right in the hard times. A student observes that kids do not know enough about their heroes. True heroes stand up to scrutiny. They also have the help of others who are good.

In another class, Leo shows PowerPoint slides of the history of superheroes. He has slides of Dr. Fate, an early superhero, then the Incredible Hulk and Batman. He asks his class, "Would you rather be a W or an IT? Would you rather be a superhero or a supervillain?" The replies from his peers are surprisingly nuanced.

Rose:	Well, I think it would be *easier* to be a supervillain. But I think it would be *better* to be a superhero. I think it would be easier to be a supervillain because, like, you just do whatever you think's wrong. And if you're a superhero, then you try to do what's right.
Brandon:	Haven?
Haven:	I'd say it is easier to be a supervillain because, like in IT's case, he can control everyone and everything. He has power over everyone in Camazotz, whereas in real life they don't really have that much control. They have control over some stuff but not that much. I'd agree it would be better to be a superhero because everyone would like you a lot more.
Rose:	Well, if you're talking like reality, it would be better to be a superhero because you have God on your side. And who can defeat God? So. I guess it really depends if you are talking about cartoons or what.
Mr. A:	Do you think that villains intentionally do the wrong thing, and that's easier than doing the right thing? [Some students say yes.] So consider IT, then, just as he was just starting Camazotz. So he was a very young brain then. Camazotz has not yet been created. Don't you think it was a lot of work for him to get to where he was if you imagine backward a little bit?
Leo:	When I was looking for trailers for the clip that I showed you of the *Avengers*, I looked at the *Batman* clip. And the villain, he made things explode a lot. And he destroyed bridges and entire football fields and high schools and things like that. And he had thousands and thousands of people. And you have to think about all of the work that went into

> getting the explosives, getting the . . . he had some high-tech ship that he
> flew around everywhere.

Student: He probably just stole them, though.

Leo: But still, to steal them!

Scott: Heroes have a lot of help. In the *Avengers* movie, they're working with the
government.

The themes of this discussion run deep: Is it easier to be good, or is it easier to be bad? What does it mean to be good versus bad? If the majority of the populace makes good choices, it might be harder and take more ingenuity to do evil. Being evil might require a work ethic and ingenious mind. Villains, like superheroes, are complex and cannot be portrayed simplistically in popular culture or literature.

Pedagogical Insight #12: Occasionally request that students deliberately make unusual claims. This stretches their thinking and can transfer into better student writing over time (authors who make unusual claims are intrinsically interesting and, if they defend their claims with warranted arguments, innovative thinkers). Using popular culture characters to make connections with literary characters helps set up unusual claims.

In one class, Matt asked students who would win in a fight: Luke Skywalker vs. IT or Mrs. W vs. Voldemort. A student observed that IT would probably win because IT could mess with Luke Skywalker's mind.

Mr. A: But Luke Skywalker triumphs over Darth Vader. Do you think IT is more
powerful than Darth Vader? [There is a chorus of yesses followed by some
no's]. Chelle, why don't you tell me the opposing side.

Chelle: Well, it's because, like, Luke is one who seems like mental attacks wouldn't
do much damage on him because he seems like someone who is . . . he's
kind of like one who is not trying to hide everything. He's kind of open to
people. So he doesn't seem like one who would suffer much with IT.

Mr. A: Especially once he becomes a Jedi, right? He's pretty mentally tough once he
becomes a Jedi. What about you guys? [pointing to a different table]

Indigo: We had Mrs. W and Voldemort. And we said Voldemort would win.

Mr. A: All right. Why?

Indigo: Because he's, like, I don't know. I've never seen *Harry Potter*. I don't know
who would win. Anyone here?

There are a lot of opinions stated, but a student finally asserts that Voldemort would win because he has magic on his side. Others note that Mrs. W does also, as she can tesser between worlds. The discussion places a literary text in conversation with other narratives of popular culture. The discussion also helps students provide objective summaries of a text and defend their responses based on evidence while making text-to-text connections.

 Pedagogical Insight #13: Student-dominated literature discussion doesn't exist in a vacuum. Instructional decision can scaffold discussion even when students aren't technically discussing literature.

Matt is adept at using technology to set up opportunities for literature discussion using popular culture. At the beginning of this unit he took his students to the computer lab, added them all to his "teacher" Pinterest page, and had them pin a picture to match characters in *A Wrinkle in Time*. Students also had to add a line of text and the page number to defend their choice. Textual evidence helped students get past appearances of characters to motivations of characters and less literal, more abstract constructions of them. Students were able to read their peers' writing and became inculcated in the ideology that everyone's voices counted in their language arts class and that the well-defended opinions of others might cause a reasonable person to change his or her mind on a topic. For example, initially Louis wrote about his current understanding of Calvin, a character in *A Wrinkle in Time*, using a line from page 31 of his book: "He's a couple of grades above me, and he's on the basketball team." He pasted a picture of a red Nike shoe to align with his quote. Students later revisited the Pinterest pages to amend their inferences about characters based on more reading. They observed that Calvin probably wouldn't be wearing fancy athletic shoes because the text observes that Calvin's family is poor and he dresses in clothes that are too small. That's the beauty of revisiting past themes in discussion and writing. Louis was thinking when he made the initial statement; his peers were thinking when they updated their textual information.

Matt employs other interactive instructional strategies to increase student comprehension of their reading and comfort and confidence to speak up in class about literature. Students participate in comprehension freeze frames in which Matt jigsaws (assigns groups pivotal and sequential incidents across chapters) and students act out those scenes without words. Students are highly engaged in this activity, and their improvisation becomes performance assessment for what students remember and misunderstood about passages. Plus, before scenes are enacted, opportunities for small-group discussion in which students talk about what confused them in *A Wrinkle in Time* are especially important because students want to perform accurately; they know that their peers will catch mistakes. Matt uses preparation time for direct instruction to discuss difficult concepts that are important for further reading (tesser, metamorphosis, changes in parts of speech, and why this happens in science fiction) even beyond this text to high school and college literature. Matt employs theatre and games to get every student comfortable speaking to a whole group in front of the classroom and to make text-to-text connections.

Matt also introduces collaborative games to encourage group cohesion so that students can form personal opinions about texts. One day he has students play at their table groups. Each table is given red and green dice to roll. Each number on the red dice represents a superhero (1 = Luke Skywalker; 2 = Harry Potter; 3 = Mrs. Whatsit; 4 = Batman; 5 = Frodo Baggins; 6 = free choice). Each number on the green dice represents a villain (1 = Darth Vader; 2 = Voldemort; 3 = IT; 4 = Joker; 5 = Sauron; 6 = free choice). Students are to respond to comprehension questions such as, who would win in a fight? And what would the fight be like? They are to justify their choices based on their understanding of the text. These instructional choices help explain why student discussions were so rich. He is asking the kinds of questions adolescents enjoy and are good at answering.

Frequently students journal and share their responses. For example, when students discuss time travel, Matt offers them several prompts to get student cognition flowing:

- If I had a time machine, I would . . .
- Time travel is possible. Here's how . . .
- Time travel is impossible. Here's why . . .
- This celebrity is actually a time traveler. Here's how you can tell . . .

Matt makes text-to-text connections of movies that feature time travel, including clips of *Napoleon Dynamite*, a clip of Bill and Ted in the phone booth with Rufus in *Bill and Ted's Excellent Adventure*, and Marty McFly in *Back to the Future*. But students are most reactive to a clip from *Phineas and Ferb*, a cartoon they watch in their immediate generation of popular culture. When students discuss the alternate realities in *A Wrinkle in Time*, Matt shows clips from *The Truman Show* to demonstrate the difficult concept.

The culminating project of this unit, once everyone has read and understood *A Wrinkle in Time*, is for students to offer celebrities struggling with advice on personal issues gleaned from the themes of the book. Their responses should show citations from the text proving they have closely read the text and can apply lessons from the text to the real world.

On the last day of the *Wrinkle in Time* unit, 10 discussion stations are placed throughout the room. Students are to travel across the stations and respond orally and then in writing as they synthesize their thoughts to a question posted at the station.

- Station 1: Evaluate *A Wrinkle in Time*. How many stars would you give it out of four?
  - What was your favorite part?
  - What was your least favorite part?
- Station 2: Which of the pop culture topics appealed to you? Why?
- Station 3: This book has had much controversy. Should it be banned?
- Station 4: What is the major theme of this book? What was the major lesson you learned?
- Station 5: Tie in the character and the lesson learned: Mrs. Murray and family, IT and love, Calvin and friendship.
- Station 6 asks the same question as station 5 but with different people.
- Station 7: Tie in the character and the lesson learned: Mr. Murray and family.
- Station 8: Apply a character and a lesson learned to people in real life.
- Station 9: Discuss a well-known person who has recently made a bad decision.
- Station 10: In your journal, describe when you made a bad decision. Select a character from *A Wrinkle in Time* who could have offered you advice before you made the decision. What advice would that character give?

Matt's penchant for emphasizing literary discussions referencing connections with popular culture works. The student vignettes offered in this book demonstrate that students are not only deeply engaged in sense-making of text and the themes of text in the real world, but they also have met Common Core standards for reading literature because of an emphasis on speaking and listening.

Throughout this unit, students have:

- Cited textual evidence to support their analysis of what the text says implicitly as well as reading between the lines.
- Determined central ideas of this text and traced that theme as they continued reading the text.
- Analyzed how elements of story grammar came together to form quality literature.
- Identified recurrent vocabulary in the text.
- Determined the genre of the text.
- Analyzed the points of view of characters.
- Supported an opinion when they have additional evidence to bring to the group.

These students are learning how to participate in democracy. In an English language arts classroom, textual discussion is a necessary instructional tool for this to happen. But successful discussion, especially student-led and student-dominated discussion, does not just happen overnight. It takes scaffolding and nurturing over time. It also takes a teacher who is willing to go there, to go deep because he or she has a pedagogy that believes that permeable discussion belongs in school and that pedagogy is carried out in instructional practices. We recommend that you articulate your pedagogy using the following reflection questions as a framework.

Opportunity for Reflection

Consider how you might apply the ideas from this chapter to your own classroom.

1. Make a video of your class engaged in a discussion. Who is asking questions: you, the teacher, or the students? What kinds of questions are they asking: literal questions with yes or no or one-word answers or open-ended questions? Then conduct a workshop on asking good questions and make a video again and again if necessary. Have the data changed? To what do you attribute this change or lack of change?

2. Train students to think in terms of what makes a generative question versus what does not. Have students explain what makes a question generative. Incorporate student questions into tests and quizzes and attribute them to students. Asking good questions is a life skill and should be appreciated and respected by group members!

3. Try referencing events in popular culture when studying literature and see if it makes a difference in the length, depth, and number of student conversational turns. Pose a question to students about a particular character. How many students respond? Now connect that character to someone similar in popular culture. Pose the same question again, but this time ask students to think about a celebrity they already know. How many students respond? Are their responses longer and deeper with more students piggybacking on each other's comments? Why or why not?

4. Cue students to deeper conversational turns by habitually asking "why" questions with regard to literary characters, setting, dialogue, conflict, and resolution. Then combine two or more aspects of story grammar (What can we infer about Character X by the way the character talks? How does Character X's personality contribute to the conflict?). Can you create two more cause-and-effect questions using story grammar elements?

5. Model to students how you make literary inferences by engaging in a think-aloud of how you are reading between the lines based on what you know about literature from other texts or your personal experience. Habitually make text-to-self, text-to-world, or text-to-text connections a classroom occurrence. Are students more likely to complete class or homework assignments about

authentic literature connections than prescribed questions at the end of a reading assignment? Why or why not? Are their responses more insightful on authentic literature connections than on prescribed questions at the end of a reading assignment? Why or why not?

6. Take an inventory of the questions you asked students to answer lately. Did you ask them to evaluate literary characters as human beings or as rarefied constructs? Do the questions you ask about literature encourage sense-making of the human condition? Why or why not?

7. Take note when side talk occurs in a whole-class discussion. Why is side talk occurring? How can you manage it constructively for deeper teaching and learning?

8. What conversational themes keep organically occurring (students bring them up) during a literary unit? How can you build on this knowledge capital in the future and turn this into part of your unit design?

9. Scan the vignettes of student talk in this chapter. How does Matt let students do the heavy thinking in this class? When does he step in and step aside?

10. Reflect on the last discussion you had with another person or group that went deep. What were the environmental conditions that made such sharing possible?

11. This next suggestion is a lot like number 3 but with a visual strategy added. Create a t-chart on a chalkboard the next time you want to compare and contrast characters. Label one side "compare" and the other "contrast." Count the number of conversational turns when comparing and contrasting two literary characters. Now compare and contrast a literary character with a figure in popular culture. How many student conversational turns occurred? To what do you attribute differences in conversational turns?

12. Set up scenarios for students where popular culture characters are pitted against literary counterparts. Cue students into making unusual claims. Is student discussion participation livelier or more detailed than in typical discussions? Does student thinking become more creative? Why or why not?

13. What activities in your class could be characterized as having close to 100 percent student engagement? Can these activities scaffold literary discussions? If not, what kinds of activities might scaffold students into feeling comfortable and insightful enough to contribute deeper conversational turns?

7 | Pop Culture and Media Literacy

There are often surprising things that happen when working with adolescents. Students in the secondary grades say and do surprising—and insightful—things. When we English language arts (ELA) teachers incorporate popular texts into literature discussions, we are taking the risk of being open to these surprising comments and insights, since each student's experience with, and interest in, popular culture is different. And, as previously mentioned, this openness to being surprised by students is often scary. But we believe that this is what adds to the richness of literature discussions. Allowing students to activate their prior knowledge in order to make connections between and among texts is where the potential for authentic learning can occur. As students reference their own knowledge, their own experiences, their own understanding of the world around them, they learn from each other *and* see the world differently. However, we need to be open for those connections and insights to occur. We need to make space for students to connect classroom literature to the texts they already know.

For example, in considering the character of Meg in *A Wrinkle in Time*, one of Matt's students, A. J., responded,

> Meg learns that you don't need to make changes to become more popular. In the book she isn't very self-confident and is unhappy with the way she is. . . . She is always trying to get rid of her faults, but then she learns how to use those faults to her advantage. . . . Lindsay Lohan should learn from Meg. . . . She [would] learn that she didn't need to do drugs and all of the things that took away her self-confidence. And she might have continued to have a more successful career.

In making the connection between the character of Meg and Lindsay Lohan, A. J. demonstrates a surprising insight into a character's *and* a celebrity's lack of self-confidence.

His knowledge of a popular text (Lindsay Lohan) allows him to make sense of a literary character (Meg), and in doing so, he offers a surprising insight while at the same time connecting the literature to what he knows. What A. J. is doing, then, is exhibiting a type of literacy that varies from academic literacy. Ernest Morrell (2004) writes, "Academic literacy . . . refers to those forms of engaging, producing, and dialoging about texts that have value in primary, secondary, and postsecondary education" (p. 11). In essence, academic literacy includes the ways we interact (read, write, speak, view) the classical, canonical texts of ELA (often referred to as "the dead white guys"). What A. J. did in Matt's classroom, however, was show that not only did he consider the literary text of the classroom through an examination of Meg's character in *A Wrinkle in Time*, but also he thought about "'the intertextuality of . . . icons . . . of media and popular culture'" (Luke qtd. in Hobbs, 2007, p. 7) through an analysis of Lindsay Lohan. A. J. used a current cultural icon (Lindsay Lohan) to understand the character of Meg from the text used in his particular academic setting. But he also used Meg to understand Lindsay Lohan. As a result, A. J. moved beyond academic literacy to another (some might say just as, or more, complex) literacy.

Defining Media Literacy

While many ELA teachers have begun to incorporate texts from popular culture into their classrooms, often that inclusion is of film adaptations of literary works read in class or of popular texts that serve as bridges or stepping stones (rap or hip hop music in a poetry unit, for example) to the literature of the ELA canon. These uses of popular culture texts are considered using popular texts in the service of academic literacy. But we think Matt's pedagogy shows surprising outcomes in that including popular culture texts in the ELA classroom can also lead to *media literacy*. David Buckingham (2003) in his book *Media Education: Literacy, Learning and Contemporary Culture* writes:

> Media *education*, then, is the process of teaching and learning about media; media *literacy* is the outcome—the knowledge and skills learners acquire . . . media literacy necessarily involves 'reading' and 'writing' media. Media education therefore aims to develop *both* critical understanding *and* active participation. It enables young people to interpret and make informed judgements as consumers of media; but it also enables them to become producers of media in their own right. Media education is about developing young people's critical and creative abilities. (p. 4, emphasis in the original)

Buckingham later writes: "The term 'media literacy' refers to the knowledge, skills and competencies that are required in order to use and interpret media" (p. 36). One of the helpful pedagogical insights Kathryn realized in her teaching and learning is that any discussion of media literacy—"'reading' and 'writing' the media"—can include not only texts from popular culture, but also texts from the classical canon. Specifically, the reading, writing, speaking, and listening skills we promote through literary discussion are also the skills we hope all ELA students apply to mass media, or popular culture, texts.

To further a consideration of media literacy and the surprising moves students make in the classroom, Renee Hobbs (2007), in her book *Reading the Media: Media Literacy in High School English,* lays out five core concepts of media literacy (p. 41):

1. All media messages are constructed.
2. Media use symbol systems with codes and conventions to shape messages.
3. Media messages have embedded values and points of view.
4. Different people interpret the same media message differently.
5. Most media messages are constructed to gain profit and/or power.

As we discussed in Chapter 4, students often hold a number of competencies regarding mass media and popular culture—often these are competencies of which both we, as ELA teachers, and they, as ELA students, are unaware. Because students (and, we would argue, teachers) are rarely asked to think about or talk about their engagement with mass media and popular culture, knowledge and skills (including understanding of Hobbs's five core concepts) are often left unexamined. But, as A. J. revealed in Matt's classroom, students, when given the opportunity, show critical understanding (knowledge and skills) and active participation (competencies) when they are able to activate their knowledge of popular texts as they discuss the academic texts (literature) of the ELA classroom.

How Media Literacy Occurs Through Discussions

Incorporating popular texts into ELA opens up avenues, often surprising avenues, of study and of discussion—avenues that lead to critical thinking about the literature of the ELA canon *and* to critical thinking about texts from popular culture. That is to say, the knowledge, skills, and competencies required to use and interpret the media (Buckingham, 2003) are the knowledge, skills, and competencies that are needed to use and interpret the texts of the ELA classroom. Now, we realize that you may be reading this chapter and thinking, "Wait a minute. I don't have time to do what I'm already required to do. There is no way I am adding a study of mass media into my curriculum!" And we are not advocating that. What we are saying is that surprising learning can, and does, occur when you open the door to activating prior knowledge and to allowing connections between literature and popular texts to occur.

Let's look at an example. Like every grade 9 teacher in the nation, Kathryn had to teach Shakespeare's *Romeo and Juliet*. And, like every grade 9 teacher in the nation, she always experienced a bit of nervousness at the beginning of the unit in thinking about how to help her students gain access to the language of the play. Thankfully, she had access to two film adaptations (by Zefferelli in 1968 and by Luhrmann in 1996) that she could use to intersperse clips in order for her students to see the play while they were reading it. But it wasn't enough to simply add the films (or clips of the films), so Kathryn had her students look for, and keep track of, decisions the writers and directors of the films made in order to adapt the play for the film medium. In doing so, Kathryn was having her students develop and expand their literacy skill of interpreting a form of mass media (film). Students had to "read" the film clips in order to discover what the filmmakers were doing; students had to understand how the film was constructed and why it was constructed (Hobbs, 2007). In doing this type of media reading, students were able to read Shakespeare's play with new, and different, eyes. In today's language of Common Core standards, Kathryn's students were analyzing "how two or more texts address similar themes or topics in order to build knowledge or to compare the approaches the authors [creators, directors] take" (CCSS.ELA-Literacy.CCRA.R.9). That is to say, as Kathryn's students studied the "language" of film, they were developing skills in media literacy; at the same time, they were applying those media literacy skills to uncover another layer of Shakespeare. Their knowledge, skills, and competencies transferred from one medium (a film adaptation) to another (Shakespeare's play). In thinking about the decisions the producers (and distributors) of the texts made, students were able to gain knowledge, skills, and competencies to make similar moves across all texts, both canonical and popular.

It's important to think about and discuss, however, the difference between using texts from popular culture in the ELA classroom and incorporating (or moving toward) media literacy. What we argue for in this book is that incorporating popular texts in discussions of literature can lead to a deeper understanding and engagement with literary texts (the canonical texts of the English language arts). As mentioned earlier, many ELA teachers use (film or television) adaptations of canonical texts as stepping stones to gain access to the literary text. The argument for this is that having students watch a film or television adaptation of a text will spark an interest to read the text. This, like using hip hop or rap songs in a poetry unit or using an episode of *The Simpsons* during a unit on satire, is understood as using texts from popular culture in the service of literary texts and is a move that can lead to vibrant discussion and understanding.

What we see in Matt's classroom, however, is that when popular texts are allowed in ELA, a surprising literacy occurs (Hobbs, 2007). Hobbs writes, "The use of digital media and popular culture texts not only stimulates young people's engagement, motivation, and interest in learning, but enables them to build a richer, more nuanced understanding of how texts of all kinds work within a culture" (p. 7). Matt's student Louis demonstrates his nuanced understanding of how texts work when he writes:

> In *A Wrinkle in Time*, Meg learned that she didn't need to change her look and personality so that people would like her. In the beginning, Meg was not a cooperative student because . . . [she] didn't have any friends at school to help her feel like she was perfect the way she already was. . . . Selena Gomez . . . was so caught up in being pretty, that she became anorexic. She felt like she needed to be like all the other celebrities and she got caught up with all of that bad stuff. Selena Gomez and Meg both thought low of themselves.

By using a popular text (Selena Gomez) to understand a literary text (*A Wrinkle in Time*), Louis demonstrates a nuanced understanding of how texts work. By juxtaposing the character of Meg with the celebrity of Selena Gomez, Louis shows that he understands that in many ways celebrities are socially created both by media producers as well as by audiences and feel pressure to meet a standardized ideal. Louis' understanding of Meg and the academic text is richer and more nuanced because of the way he was able to make connections to a text (Selena Gomez) he already knew. Louis can see in Meg the same type of insecurity and desire to be liked and accepted that he sees in a celebrity. In this way, Louis has applied what he has "learned in a variety of new contexts . . . [and can] see connections between ideas and information" (Hobbs, p. 8)—media literacy skills that can both improve and enhance academic literacy skills.

Ways to Help Students Understand How Mass Media Work

As we consider incorporating popular culture texts with academic literary texts, we need to pause to consider what such incorporation might mean. Sometimes using the film adaptation of a literary text is enough; sometimes there is only time for that. But, as we have shown, using popular texts in literary discussion offers significant potential for connections between and among texts—connections that can lead to surprising learning and understanding. Thus, studying—learning about—the way that texts are distributed through mass media is equally important. While many ELA teachers pair the film adaptation of a piece of literature, we think an important part of this pairing is for students to learn, even briefly, how film (or any other mass medium) works in order to understand the decisions the creators of the film made to communicate the story of the film. In this way, students will then be able to have conversations about the decisions that authors make to communicate what they have written. It is this type of questioning and excavation that can lead to a rich understanding of mass media, popular texts, and literature. For example, when Kathryn was teaching *To Kill a Mockingbird* in a grade 10 literature course, and after watching the 1962 film adaptation of the novel, she had her students think about, and research, not only the decisions that went into making both the book and the film, but also the decisions that went into distributing the book and the film and keeping both part of the American literary canon. Kathryn asked her students to consider questions like: .

- Who decided that this is a book that almost every grade 10 student should read?
- What are the characteristics of the novel that make it popular?
- What are the characteristics of the novel that make it popular in educational settings (for teachers, principals, school boards, and federal testing organizations)?
- Who says that this is an important literary text to read? Who are "they"?
- What changes to the story, characters, or setting did the filmmakers incorporate?
  - Why were these changes made?
  - How do the changes affect an understanding of the novel?
- Why has the film remained so popular for so many years?

These are the questions that can, and do, lead to class discussions that "analyze the structure of texts, including how specific sentences, paragraphs, and larger portions of the text (e.g., a section, chapter, scene, stanza) relate to each other and the whole" (CCSS.ELA-Literacy.CCRA.R.5). As students analyze film adaptations (popular texts) at the same time they are analyzing literary texts, they are relating parts to each other (film scene to film scene, film scene to novel scene), relating parts to the whole (scene to scene, film to novel), relating adaptation to text, and relating text(s) to other larger concepts. As such, students are developing critical understanding and active participation; they are interpreting the construction of messages, conventions, and points of view; they are revealing the knowledge, skills, and competencies they use to interpret media and literary texts.

It's important to reiterate at this point that we aren't necessarily trying to convince you to incorporate media literacy into your ELA classroom. We know how overwhelming it feels when we teachers are asked to add on yet one more text, assignment, topic, conversation, and so on. What we are hoping to do, however, is to encourage you to take some time to notice what you and your students are *already* doing as you interact with and engage popular texts. What we are trying to do is have you become aware of the prior knowledge and skills students are activating (or are trying to do so) in discussions of literary texts. What we hope you will do is to take a chance on incorporating a popular text into a discussion of a literary text. We trust that if you take one or two of these small steps, you'll be surprised by the insights and abilities of your students. Matt's students, through his willingness to allow them to connect the literary text of *A Wrinkle in Time* with popular texts, were able to gain a wide range knowledge, skills, and competencies as their connections between the literary text and popular texts opened new avenues of consideration. As Matt's student James demonstrates:

> In *A Wrinkle in Time*, Charles Wallace learns the importance of listening and taking advice, and the dangers of being arrogant. Throughout the book, we learn that Charles is brilliant, but also very arrogant. The three Mrs. W's caution him to 'be aware of pride and arrogance.'. . . Not listening to anybody's advice, Charles gets into trouble. He becomes hypnotized by the Man with the Red Eyes, thinking he was strong enough to handle it on his own. His failure to listen and his exaggerated perception of his abilities did not allow him to withstand evil. [Tiger Woods] could learn from Charles. . . . Because of his amazing ability at golf, Tiger because very arrogant and thought he could do anything that he pleased without consequences. He cheated on his wife with multiple women and ended up with a ruined reputation. He lost many sponsors and longtime fans, and his golf game suffered. . . . Tiger Woods . . . could have learned from Charles that his talents alone are not enough . . . and that he should be less arrogant.

As an unintended consequence of allowing popular culture texts to be a large part of his class's literary reading and literary discussion, Matt found that his students were more reflective and analytical of popular texts—reflective and analytical in a way that he was teaching them to be with academic texts. Simply, Matt's students were becoming more media literate because they were given the space to think about and discuss the connections between texts of the literary canon and texts from popular culture.

Putting It All Together

So, can Shakespeare and popular culture exist in the same classroom? We think that they can and that often they do. But this relationship between popular texts and literary texts feels, sometimes, uncomfortable. Many times we, as ELA teachers, feel like we are cheating on the literary canon when we allow popular texts to enter into conversations we have with students. We feel unfaithful to the high cultural standards we are used to as former English majors and scholars. We feel that using popular culture lowers the standards we have for our students and ourselves or, at the most basic level, causes others to see us as having lower standards.

This doesn't need to be the case. As Matt and his students have demonstrated to us, the incorporation of popular texts can enhance and increase students' engagement with literary texts. As students have the time and space to explore the knowledge, skills, and competencies they are already using as they interact with popular texts, they practice and develop the knowledge, skills, and competencies they need for success with academic, literary texts. As Morrell (2004) argues, "Developing a broad conceptual framework for popular culture . . . will help teachers . . . [recast] popular culture as the representation of everyday activity. This recasting also repositions young people as producers and participants in popular culture, rather than as passive consumers of popular culture" (p. 35). Morrell also writes, "[Once] students have learned to make sense of the texts that permeate their own world, they will be better able to engage the texts that represent the languages, cultures, and experiences of the worlds distant and past" (p. 43).

Opportunity for Reflection

Consider how you might apply the ideas from this chapter to your own classroom.

1. How would you define media literacy in your own words?

2. Have you taught media literacy in the past? Explain. What worked and what would you do differently in the future?

3. How might you use film and text pairings to promote media literacy? What kinds of questions could you ask students to help them compare the film and print versions? What kinds of activities could you assign?

4. What are some other ways to help students understand mass media and literacy (besides film pairings)?

5. What are the first steps you will take after reading this book to begin incorporating pop culture into your class discussions? Your first steps can be small and short-term or broader and more long-term.

References

Adorno, T., & Horkheimer, M. (1944/2001). The culture industry: Enlightenment as mass deception. In M.G. Durham & D.M. Kellner (Eds.), *Media and cultural studies: Keyworks* (pp. 71–101). Malden, MA: Blackwell Publishers.

Allender, D. (2004). Popular culture in the classroom. *English Journal, 93*, 12–14.

Almasi, J. (1995). The nature of fourth-graders' sociocognitive conflicts in peer-led and teacher-led discussions of literature. *Reading Research Quarterly, 30*, 314–351.

Asselin, M. (2001). Teaching literacy from and with popular culture. *Teacher Librarian, 28*, 47–49.

Aukerman, M. (2008). In praise of wiggle room: Locating comprehension in unlikely places. *Language Arts, 86*, 52–60.

Barnes, D. (1993). Supporting exploratory talk for learning. In K. M. Pierce & C. J. Giles (Eds.), *Cycles of meaning: Exploring the potential of talk in learning communities* (pp. 17–34). Portsmouth, NH: Heinemann.

Barrentine, S. J. (1996). Engaging with reading through interactive read-alouds. *Reading Teacher, 50*, 36–43.

Barton, D., Hamilton, M., & Ivanic, R. (2000). *Situated literacies: Reading and writing in context*. NewYork: Routledge.

Benjamin, W. (1936/2001). The work of art in the age of mechanical reproduction. In M.G. Durham & D.M. Kellner (Eds.), *Media and cultural studies: Keyworks* (pp. 48–70). Malden, MA: Blackwell Publishers.

Berger, J. (1972). *Ways of seeing*. London: Penguin Books.

Bucholtz, M., & Hall, K. (2005). Identity and interaction: A sociocultural linguistic approach. *Discourse Studies, 7*, 585–614.

Buckingham, D. (2003). *Media education: Literacy, learning and contemporary culture*. Cambridge, UK: Polity Press.

Cawelti, J.G. (2004). *Mystery, violence, and popular culture*. Madison: University of Wisconsin Press.

Cazden, C. B. (2001). *Classroom discourse: The language of teaching and learning* (2nd ed.). Portsmouth, NH: Heinemann.

Dewey, J. (1934). *Art as experience*. New York: Perigee Books.

Diehl, H. L. (2005). Snapshots of our journey to thoughtful literacy. *ReadingTeacher, 59*, 56–69.

duGay, P., Hall, S., Janes, L., Mackay, H., & Negus, K. (1997). *Doing cultural studies: The story of the Sony Walkman*. London: Sage Publications.

Durham, M.G., & Kellner, D.M. (2001). Adventures in media and cultural studies: Introducing the key works. In Authors (Eds.), *Media and cultural studies: Keyworks* (pp. 1–30). Malden, MA: Blackwell Publishers.

Dyson, A. H. (1997). *Writing superheroes: Contemporary childhood, popular culture, and classroom literacy*. New York: Teachers College Press.

Dyson, A. H. (2003). *The brothers and sisters learn to write: Popular literacies in childhood and school cultures*. New York: Teachers College Press.

Eeds, M., & Wells, D. (1989). Grand conversations: An exploration of meaning construction in literature study groups. *Research in the Teaching of English, 23*, 4–29.

Gee, J. P. (1996). *Sociolinguistics and literacies: Ideology in discourses*. Bristol, PA: Taylor & Francis.

Golden, J.M. (2001). Reader-text interaction. *Theory into Practice, 24*, 91–96.

Gritter, K. (2010). Promoting lively literature discussion. *Reading Teacher, 64*, 445–449.

Gritter, K. (2012). Permeable textual discussion in tracked language arts classrooms. *Research in the Teaching of English, 46*, 232–259.

Guins, R., & Cruz, O.Z. (2005). *Popular culture: A reader*. London: Sage Publications.

Hagood, M.C., Alvermann, D.E., & Heron-Hruby, A. (2010). *Bring it to class: Unpacking pop culture in literacy learning*. New York: Teachers College Press.

Hartup, W. W. (1996). Cooperation, close relationships, and cognitive development. In W. M. Bukowski, A. F. Newcomb, & W. W. Hartup (Eds.), *The company they keep: Friendship in childhood and adolescence* (pp. 213–237). Cambridge, UK: Cambridge University Press.

Harvey, D., & Bizar, M. (1998). *Methods that matter: Six structures for best practice classrooms*. Portland, ME: Steinhouse.

Hawkins, M. R. (Ed.). (2004). *Language learning and teacher education*. Buffalo, NY: Multilingual Matters.

Hobbs, R. (1998). Literacy in the information age. In J. Flood, D. Lapp, & S. Brice-Heath (Eds.), *Handbook of research on teaching literacy through the communicative and visual arts* (pp. 7–14). New York: Macmillan.

Hobbs, R. (2007). *Reading the media: Media literacy in high school English*. New York: Teachers College Press.

Hobbs, R., & Frost, R. (2003). Measuring the acquisition of media literacy skills. *Reading Research Quarterly, 38*, 330–355.

Hunt, T. J., & Hunt, B. (2004). New voices. *English Journal, 93*, 80–83.

Keene, E., & Zimmerman, S. (1997). *Mosaic of thought: Teaching comprehension in a reader's workshop*. Portsmouth: NH: Heinemann.

Langer, J. A. (1990). The process of understanding: Reading for literary and informative purposes. *Research in the Teaching of English, 24*, 229–260.

Langer, J. A. (2001). Beating the odds: Teaching middle and high school students to read and write well. *American Educational Research Journal, 38*, 837–880.

Leavis, F. R. (1930/2005). Mass civilisation and minority culture. In R. Guins & O. Z. Cruz (Eds.), *Popular culture: A reader* (pp. 33–38). London: Sage Publications.

Macdonald, D. (1957/2005). A theory of mass culture. In R. Guins & O. Z. Cruz (Eds.), *Popular culture: A reader* (pp. 39–46). London: Sage Publications.

Mahiri, J. (2001). Pop culture pedagogy and the end(s) of school. *Journal of Adolescent and Adult Literacy, 44*, 382–385.

Maloch, B. (2002). Scaffolding student talk: One teacher's role in literature discussion groups. *Reading Research Quarterly, 37*, 94–112.

Maloch, B., & Beutel, D. D. (2010). "Big loud voice. You have important things to say": The nature of student initiations during one teacher's interactive read-alouds. *Journal of Classroom Interaction, 45*, 20–29.

McCarthey, S. J., & Moje, E. B. (2002). Identity matters. *Reading Research Quarterly, 37*, 228–241.

McIntyre, E. (2007). Story discussion in the primary grades: Balancing authenticity and explicit teaching. *Reading Teacher, 60*, 610–620.

McLuhan, M. (1967). *The medium is the massage: An inventory of effects*. Corte Madera, CA: Gingko Press.

Morgan, W. (1998). Critical literacy. In W. Sawyer, K. Watson, & E. Gold (Eds.), *Re-viewing English* (pp. 154–163). Sydney, AU: St. Clair Press.

Morocco, C. C., & Hindin, A. (2002). The role of conversation in a thematic understanding of literature. *Learning Disabilities Research & Practice, 17*, 144–159.

Morrell, E. (2002). Toward a critical pedagogy of popular culture: Literacy development among urban youth. *Journal of Adolescent and Adult Literacy, 46*, 72–77.

Morrell, E. (2004). *Linking literacy and popular culture: Finding connections for lifelong learning*. Norwood, MA: Christopher-Gordon Publishers.

New London Group. (1996). A pedagogy of multiliteracies: Designing social futures. *Harvard Educational Review, 66*, 60–92.

Nye, R. (1970). *The unembarrassed muse: The popular arts in America*. New York: Dial Press.

Nystrand, M. (1997). *Opening dialogue: Understanding the dynamics of language and learning in the English classroom*. New York: Teachers College Press.

Paley, V. (1997). *The girl with the brown crayon: How children use stories to shape their lives*. Cambridge, MA: Harvard University Press.

Palincsar, A. S., & Brown, A. L. (1984). Reciprocal teaching of comprehension-fostering and comprehension-monitoring activities. *Cognition & Instruction, 1*, 117–175.

Pressley, M., Roehrig, A., Bogner, K., Raphael, L. M., & Dolezal, S. (2002). Balanced literacy instruction. *Focus on Exceptional Children, 34*, 1–14.

Purcell-Gates, V. (1991). On the outside looking in: A study of remedial readers' meaning-making while reading literature. *Journal of Reading Behavior: A Journal of Literacy, 23*, 235–253.

Rosenblatt, L. M. (1968). *Literature as Exploration*.Champaign, IL: National Council of Teachers of English.

Schoon-Tanis, K. (2010). *Wait, I can use that in my classroom?! Popular culture in/and secondary English language arts* (Published dissertation). East Lansing, MI.

Shiach, M. (1989/2005). The popular. In R. Guins & O. Z. Cruz (Eds.), *Popular culture: A reader* (pp. 55–64). London: Sage Publications.

Storey, J. (1996). *Cultural studies and the study of popular culture: Theories and methods*. Athens: University of Georgia Press.

Storey, J. (2003). *Inventing popular culture*. Malden, MA: Blackwell.

Storey, J. (2006). Introduction: the study of popular culture and cultural studies. In J. Storey (Ed.), *Cultural theory and popular culture (a reader)* (3rd ed., pp. xv–xxii). Harlow, England: Pearson Education Limited.

Strinati, D. (1995). *An introduction to theories of popular culture*. London: Routledge.

Vygotsky, L. S. (1978). *Mind in society: The development of higher psychological processes* (M. Cole, V. John-Steiner, S. Scribner, & E. Souberman, Eds. & Trans.). Cambridge, MA: Harvard University Press. (Original work published 1934).

Williams, R. (1976/2005). Culture and masses. In R. Guins & O. Z. Cruz (Eds.), *Popular culture: A reader* (pp. 25–32). London: Sage Publications.

Wilson, J. L., & Laman, T. T. (2007). "That was basically me": Critical literacy, text, and talk. *Voices from the Middle, 15*, 40–46.

Worthham, S. (2004). The interdependence of social identification and learning. *American Educational Research Journal, 41*, 715–750.

Yalom, I. D. (1995). *The theory and practice of group psychotherapy* (4th ed.). New York: Basic Books.